$20.00

The Yale Library of Milit   _ ,

Donald Kagan and Frederick Kagan, Series Editors

THE
UNKNOWN
BATTLE OF MIDWAY

THE DESTRUCTION OF THE
AMERICAN TORPEDO SQUADRONS

ALVIN KERNAN

Foreword by DONALD KAGAN and FREDERICK KAGAN

Yale University Press / New Haven and London

Published with assistance from the foundation established in memory of
Philip Hamilton McMillan of the Class of 1894, Yale College.

Designed by Mary Valencia.
Set in Minion type by Tseng Information Systems, Inc.
Printed in the United States of America by R. R. Donnelley,
Harrisonburg, Virginia.

The Library of Congress has cataloged the hardcover edition as follows:
Kernan, Alvin B.
The unknown Battle of Midway : the destruction of the American
torpedo squadrons / Alvin Kernan.
p.   cm. — (Yale library of military history)
Includes bibliographical references and index.
ISBN 0-300-10989-x (clothbound : alk. paper)
1. Midway, Battle of, 1942. 2. Torpedo bombers—United States—
History—20th century. 3. World War, 1939–1945—20th century.
I. Title. II. Series.
D774.M5K47 2005
940.54′26699—dc22   2005007314

A catalogue record for this book is available from the British Library.

The paper in this book meets the guidelines for permanence and
durability of the Committee on Production Guidelines for Book Longevity
of the Council on Library Resources.

ISBN 978-0-300-12264-0 (pbk. : alk. paper)

10 9 8 7 6 5 4 3 2 1

Dedicated to the memory of
John C. Waldron, Navy Cross
Lieutenant Commander, USN
Killed in action commanding Torpedo Squadron Eight
at the Battle of Midway, June 4, 1942

CONTENTS

CONTENTS

FOREWORD

War has been a subject of intense interest from the beginning of literature around the world. Whether it be in the earliest literary work in the Western tradition, Homer's *Iliad,* or the Rigvedic hymns of ancient India, people have always been fascinated by this dangerous and challenging phenomenon. Few can fail to be stirred by such questions as: How and why do wars come about? How and why do they end? Why did the winners win and the losers lose? How do leaders make life-and-death decisions? Why do combatants follow orders that put their lives at risk? How do individuals and societies behave in war, and how are they affected by it? Recent events have raised the study of war from one of intellectual interest to a matter of vital importance to America and the world. Ordinary citizens must understand war in order to choose their leaders wisely, and leaders must understand it if they are to prevent wars where possible and win them when necessary.

This series, therefore, seeks to present the keenest analyses of war in its different aspects, the sharpest evaluations of political and military decision-making, and descriptive accounts of military activity that illuminate its human elements. It will do so drawing on the full range of military history from ancient times to the present and in every part of the globe in order to make available to the general public readable and accurate

scholarly accounts of this most fascinating and dangerous of
human activities.

Alvin Kernan, the author of *The Unknown Battle of Midway,*
is a teacher and scholar of great experience and outstanding
talent who has made a great name for himself in both fields at
Yale and Princeton. In June 1942, however, he was a young member of the crew on one of the aircraft carriers in the task force
led by Admiral Raymond Spruance that won the Battle of Midway and turned the tide against Japan in World War II.

His new book is a model of scholarship of an unusual kind.
The Unknown Battle of Midway is the clearest and most persua-
sive story of the Battle of Midway we have ever read or heard.
It asks the right questions directly and answers them clearly,
simply, and convincingly, basing its conclusions on keen analysis of the primary sources and much new evidence rarely if ever
used by other accounts. Kernan brings the events to life as only
a participant with high literary talents can. As a professional
seaman he explains the arcane details of carrier warfare to the
layman with unexampled clarity and economy. He tells us what
we need to know to understand the course of events but no
more. Beneath his calm and measured style his dismay at the
inadequacies of American preparation, failures of leadership,
and refusal to admit responsibility for these is inescapable. In
convincing detail Kernan shows the crucial role of sheer luck in
the American victory and that unpreparedness and incompe-
tence nearly produced a very different outcome. But this book,

even as it makes its powerful case, is not about finger-pointing. It is a compelling narrative that portrays real people and engages readers' hearts at the same time as it sharpens their comprehension of the events and their meaning.

Donald Kagan and Frederick Kagan

PREFACE

The famous victory at Midway of the Americans over the Japanese in early June 1942 was one of the great battles in which empires rose and fell on the fate of their ships at sea: the Spanish Armada, Trafalgar, Jutland, Midway. Midway also belongs to a special group of epic sea battles in which the western world confronted the expanding forces of Asia, at Salamis, Lepanto, Tsushima, Midway. It is the greatest battle the American navy has fought and is rightly celebrated as one of the high points of American arms. So brightly has the victory shone, however, that it has obscured how near a thing it was and how costly were our blunders. Rear Admiral Frank Jack Fletcher, who commanded the American fleet at Midway, knew better than many what had actually taken place, and he assessed it accurately when he said, "After a battle is over, people talk a lot about how the decisions were methodically reached, but actually there's always a hell of a lot of groping around" (Lord, *Incredible Victory,* 87).

That "groping around" is the raw action of all battles, and at Midway it took some remarkable twists and turns, none more tragic than the great blunders that sent four squadrons of unprepared pilots and obsolete torpedo planes against the enemy on June 4, 1942, between the hours of 7 and 11 in the morning. These blunders, the kindest word I can use, are the subject of this book, which will assemble all the pieces for the first time to reveal the total picture and expose the cover-up that concealed what actually happened.

One group, Torpedo Squadron Eight (VT-8) from the *Hornet,* has been singled out for fame, having only one survivor, the famous Ensign George Gay, who lived until 1995. But there were three other American torpedo groups at Midway: Torpedo Squadron Three (VT-3), originally a *Saratoga* squadron flying from the *Yorktown;* Torpedo Squadron Six (VT-6) from the *Enterprise;* and a mixed group of torpedo-carrying army and navy planes based on Midway Island, which I shall call the "Midway Squadron." They went in, separately, one squadron after another, on the morning of June 4, and in all, fifty-one planes tried to hit the Japanese ships with torpedoes that day. Only seven landed back at base. This comes to an aircraft loss rate of over 86 percent. Out of 128 pilots and crew who were in the torpedo planes that day, 29 survived, 99 died. And not one torpedo exploded against the hull of a Japanese ship. The battle ran on fitfully for two more days, but it was all over for the torpedo squadrons shortly after 1030 on the fourth, as it was for the Japanese carrier force when our dive-bombers got to them a few minutes later.

The record is known and honored, but the full story of what a desperately bad hand the torpedo planes played out to its bitter end has never been assembled to be read as a single story. Midway has had its historians, and fine ones too, from Samuel Eliot Morrison, Walter Lord, and Gordon Prange to John Lundstrom, but the official version has remained that the torpedo squadrons at Midway were lost making a gallant attack that cleared the upper air of Japanese fighter planes and made it possible for our dive-bombers to come in unopposed and sink the Japanese carriers. This was, unintentionally on anyone's part, admirals or torpedo pilots, part of what happened; the truth is that these squadrons, like the British Light Brigade at Balaclava in the Crimean War, never had a chance. Our torpedo planes were obsolete, whereas the Japanese fighters that shot them down were among the best in the world. Our weapon, the Mark 13, Mod. 1, aerial torpedo, failed to run hot and true much of the time, and when it hit, it often failed to explode. Because of these torpedo deficiencies, a suicidal and counterproductive drop tactic had been developed to try to prevent damage to their working parts. Because of cost during a time of tight budgets and a torpedo shortage going into the war, most of the pilots who flew in the torpedo attack at Midway had never been trained to carry and launch a "tin fish." Because of command failures and poor communications, the vulnerable torpedo planes were sent unescorted by fighters into battle, and the enemy was not diverted by simultaneous dive-bombing attacks. None of these failures, I repeat, was intentional. They were the result of bad luck and poor planning, along with an unwillingness to accept and act on the truth of what was known about our plane and its torpedo. Instead, people who knew better, acted as if everything was all right. In conjunction, these failures made for an overwhelming disaster, which, after the battle, was covered up to save careers and avoid tarnishing a big victory at a time when the American public badly wanted good news.

Midway was a multiphase battle fought with complex hardware. Understanding what happened to the torpedo squadrons requires some knowledge about the various elements involved. This information is ancient history by now, but I hope the reader will bear with me as I explain World War II aircraft carriers, airplanes, naval careers, and torpedoes, to the end of clarifying the fate of the torpedo squadrons.

I played a small part in this action, I am proud to say. I was an enlisted man, an aviation ordnanceman, eighteen years old, in Torpedo Squadron Six on board the *Enterprise,* one of three American aircraft carriers of the *Yorktown* class that fought the battle and ultimately prevailed. Small as my involvement was, it was sufficient to make me feel that I am fulfilling a duty to my shipmates in recording just how badly things went wrong for the aerial torpedo squadrons that day over the blue waters of the mid-Pacific.

Time was a critical factor in the Battle of Midway, as it is in all battles, but here the contestants used different clocks. The Americans operated on Greenwich Zone + 10, whereas the Japanese used their Tokyo home port time, Zone − 9. Because the battle was fought across the 180th degree of longitude, the International Date Line, the antagonists sometimes even used different days of the week and month. In the interest of clarity and consistency I have silently changed all times in the battle to Midway time, which is Greenwich Zone + 12, half way around the world.

The Unknown Battle of Midway

ONE

The Destruction of the American
Battle Line at Pearl Harbor

On the morning of December 7, 1941, the Imperial Japanese Navy made a surprise attack on the American Pacific Fleet tied up in Pearl Harbor at Ford Island, the pearl at the center of the deep inlet. At the naval yard, aft of a huge dry dock containing the battleship *Pennsylvania,* were the cruiser *Helena* and the minesweeper *Oglala.* Japanese intelligence had predicted that the aircraft carrier *Enterprise* would be in this position on December 7, and a torpedo intended for her smashed into the smaller ships. But the *Enterprise* and the two other American carriers then in the Pacific, *Lexington* and *Saratoga,* were not in Pearl Harbor, where Japanese intelligence had predicted they would be. The attackers knew that the carriers' absence qualified their victory enormously, and they were dead right.

Little official information about the extent of the damage in Pearl was given to those of us on the *Enterprise,* just outside the harbor, but scuttlebutt, the navy rumor mill, piled it high. Even so, when the *Enterprise* entered the harbor to refuel, late in the afternoon of December 8, we were flabbergasted by the devastation we saw as we proceeded to our dock, moving slowly around the harbor from east to west. One battleship, the *Nevada,* was lying athwart the narrow entrance channel, beached bow first, allowing barely enough room for the carrier to squeeze by and move past the great battle fleet lying in ruins at its anchorages alongside Ford Island. The water was covered with oil, fires were burning still, ships were resting on the bottom mud, superstructures had broken and fallen. Great gaps loomed where magazines had exploded, and smoke was roiling up everywhere. For sailors who had considered these massive ships invincible, it was a sight to be seen but not comprehended, and as we made our way to a dock on the west side of Ford Island, just beyond the old target battleship *Utah,* turned turtle, we seemed to be mourners at a spectacular funeral.

The navy assumed that in the event of war our battle fleet, centered on its massive battleships, would sweep across the Pacific to relieve General Douglas MacArthur and the army in the Philippines, and then beat up on the Japanese navy and go on up to Tokyo. Something like this had actually been projected for years in a series of secret war plans brightly labeled Orange and Rainbow. But it was not to be. For the time being the navy fought a holding action.

The *Saratoga* was torpedoed in January near the Hawaiian coast, and after that America, with two oceans to fight in, had only three carriers in the Pacific, the *Enterprise,* the *Yorktown,* and the *Lexington,* while the Japanese had six fleet carriers and a number of smaller ones. It was risky to go anywhere west of Hawaii, and Vice Admiral Chester Nimitz, commander in chief of the Pacific Fleet (Cincpac), played his cards carefully even after the *Yorktown* and the brand-new *Hornet,* sister ships of the *Enterprise,* came around from the Atlantic. There was, too, it has to be admitted, something of a shell-shocked sluggishness in the American fleet after Pearl Harbor. We had thought the Japanese manufactured only cheap goods you bought in ten-cent stores, but now we became acquainted with their superb optics, the devastating Zero fighter, and what was later called the Long Lance torpedo. It took only a little while to learn that the Japanese were also first-rate in their courage and in their training, and that they were unsurpassed not only in gunnery and some actions like fighting their ships at night but, most significantly for our immediate futures, in their magnificent aerial torpedo system.

The crews chafed as the American aircraft carriers operating in task forces with fast cruisers and destroyers were sent to the South Pacific to block a Japanese invasion of Australia and were limited to a series of raids, quick in, quick out, against isolated Japanese bases far out in the Pacific: Marcus, Wake, Kwajalein. We were not at the beginning really ready for war, and these raids punctuating long days of cruising taught us the skills that would enable us to win, with the aid of some good luck, the Battle of Midway. It was amazing how long it took to get the hang of it and to react instantly in the right way. War, we gradually learned, is a state of mind before it can be anything else.

The run in to an island would begin at high speed the night before a raid, and the crew sweated in their bunks all night long while the driveshafts turning at high speed rattled everything. Flight Quarters came before daylight, and soon afterward General Quarters was sounded. The ship turned into the wind to add near 30 knots plus the wind to the speed of the planes taking off. The first planes off were the fighters for the combat air patrol (CAP) overhead and then the scout planes of the anti-submarine patrol (ASP) to fly vectors looking for enemy ships or subs. The radar antenna—one thing we had, courtesy of the British, that the Japanese did not—like a double-bed spring rotated constantly on the mast top. Early radar was short-range and quirky, but it gave us a distinct advantage in knowing when unidentified planes were approaching.

Vice Admiral Chuichi Nagumo, leader of the Pearl Harbor strike and of *Kido Butai,* the Japanese fleet of aircraft carriers at Midway, and his commander in chief, Admiral Isoroku Yamamoto, were proud Japanese samurai, and while we were making small raids, they were ranging over half the world. After devastating the Pacific Fleet at Pearl Harbor, the Japanese empire went on in six months to destroy British naval power in the Far East by sinking the warships *Prince of Wales* and *Repulse* off Malaysia, capture Singapore, raid Ceylon, and obliterate a combined Australian, Dutch, and American fleet off Indonesia, bringing down the old colonial empires of Britain and the Netherlands. Japanese troops were halfway across China, had stalemated the Russians in Manchuria, and soon forced Bataan and the fortress of Corregidor to surrender in the Philippines. And now, in early June 1942, the navy was preparing to bring its ships to Midway Island, the westernmost American outpost remaining in the Pacific, with the intention of extending Japan's conquest to within 1,200 miles of Hawaii and drawing out and sinking any opposing American fleet. It was also said that the Japanese navy was so deeply embarrassed by the Doolittle Raid on Tokyo, in sight of the emperor's palace, in mid-April 1942 that it was determined to make sure that the U.S. Navy could never approach Japan again.

The Japanese navy had begun to push in late April and May toward New Guinea and Australia to the south, and the Solomon Islands and Fiji to the east, with the aim of cutting off the United States from our allies down under, Australia and New Zealand. Task Force Seventeen, commanded by Rear Admiral Frank Jack Fletcher, built around the two carriers *Yorktown* and the old warhorse the *Lexington,* stopped the Japanese drive, sinking one small carrier and putting a larger one out of commission. But the *Lexington* was sunk in the exchange and the *Yorktown* was heavily damaged. When the *Enterprise* and *Hornet,* Task Force Sixteen, arrived too late to get into the fight, the three remaining carriers were ordered to make a fast run back to Pearl Harbor.

The *Enterprise* and *Hornet* arrived back in Pearl Harbor on May 26. On May 27, the *Yorktown* returned from the Coral Sea and soon went into dry dock. The navy yard worked miracles on it, repairing in three days enough of the damage to make it possible for it to fight at Midway. All liberty was canceled, and re-provisioning and refueling of the ships began immediately. Our admiral on the "Big E," William Halsey, had been tormented with a terrible allergic rash and was forced to go into the hospital. He was relieved as commander of Task Force Sixteen by Rear Admiral Raymond Spruance, a line officer, not an aviator, who had been in command of a cruiser force.

Rumors began to circulate that the Japanese were planning to invade little Midway Atoll and draw our ships out to fight the great sea battle their strategy had long anticipated. Our information, we heard, at the scuttlebutt, came from code breakers: "Like troglodytes, [the code breakers] inhabited a kind of underworld cellar, approached only by two locked doors and in a permanent state of shabby disorder amid which heaped files and the ejections of IBM machines struggled—as the occupants were indeed doing—for survival. [Commander Joseph] Rochefort presided, in his ancient red smoking jacket and carpet slippers: a man driving himself to the limit on two or three hours of sleep and a diet of coffee and sandwiches. He slept on a cot among the squalor and had to be expelled to take a bath. A perfectionist, he allowed no message to leave Hypo [Hawaiian Code Center] until he himself had checked the translation."[1]

Unbelievably, the Japanese never tumbled throughout the entire war to the fact that their codes had been broken, and the U.S. Navy, equally blindly, continued to believe that its ability to read one after another of the Japanese codes remained a deep, dark secret from its own sailors. But when the American carriers sailed from Pearl Harbor to the Battle of Midway everyone aboard knew what was in the wind and how we knew it.

Naval Intelligence long persisted in asserting that no one other than senior officers in the fleet could have known before the battle of the breaking of the Japanese Purple Code and the impending clash at Midway. The truth was at long last brought out and established in a BOMRT (Battle of Midway Round Table) online exchange in August 2005, in which various veterans recalled how the information spread. It developed that Cincpac, at Nimitz's direction, had sent a top-secret code ULTRA message describing the Japanese plans and their ships to all senior officers in mid-May 1942. As the *Yorktown* returned from the Coral Sea, Admiral Fletcher shared his knowledge with all his officers. The information was later distributed in a "noncodeword summary" to all involved in the battle. Most tellingly, perhaps, Dan Kaseberg, a yeoman in Torpedo Squadron Three, remembers getting and posting the order of battle while on Oahu, because when he abandoned the sinking *Yorktown,* he found a copy "on oil soaked onionskin paper" in his pocket.

Admiral Nagumo may have told his carrier sailors that "the enemy lacks the will to fight," but the American navy had been making itself ready for years to fight this, its greatest sea battle.[2]

TWO

Trading Armor for Speed:
The New Battle Line

There is something in a naval engagement which radically distinguishes it from one on the land. The ocean, at times, has what is called its sea and its trough of the sea; but it has neither rivers, woods, banks, towns, nor mountains. In mild weather, it is one hammered plain. Stratagems, — like those of disciplined armies, ambuscades — like those of Indians, are impossible. All is clear, open, fluent. The very element which sustains the combatants, yields at the stroke of a feather. One wind and one tide operate upon all who here engage. This simplicity renders a battle between two men-of-war, with their huge white wings, more akin to the Miltonic contests of archangels than to the comparatively squalid tussles of earth.

So our great American sailor-writer, Herman Melville, described in *Israel Potter* (1854) the nature of naval warfare as it was conceived and practiced until December 7, 1941, and the Japanese attack on Pearl Harbor. The American and Japanese aircraft carriers that steamed to the Battle of Midway left behind them in the fires and wreckage of Pearl Harbor not just a fleet of devastated ironclads but an ancient mode of naval warfare in which for centuries battleship had thundered broadsides against battleship. Now aircraft carriers would be able to ambush unsuspecting enemies, and the crucial question for naval commanders from Pearl Harbor on had to be, "Where are the enemy carriers?"

Admiral Nimitz well understood the new strategy and tactics that December 7 enforced. Some of the Pearl Harbor battleships had been repaired by the time of Midway and were assembled in San Francisco harbor, raring to go, but Nimitz left them there, to their great chagrin. They were, he knew, too slow to keep up with 30-knot carrier task forces for one thing, but he also understood that their day had passed. They would serve in the long war to come for bombardment of assault beaches, and they slugged it out once in the Philippines in late October 1944 with equally obsolescent Japanese battleships. But the Pacific war featured fleet carrier task force against fleet carrier task force, and this type of warfare would first be displayed in its full dimensions at the Battle of the Coral Sea in May 1942, and then at Midway one month later.

Though he had designed the Pearl Harbor attack that initiated carrier war, Admiral Yamamoto, commander of the Imperial Japanese Combined Fleet, never entirely understood the lesson he had taught. At Midway, which was also very much his operation, he continued to treat his carriers as an advance force for the big-gun fleet he commanded from his flagship, the largest battleship in the world, the *Yamato*, named for the ancient Japanese kingdom. It weighed 63,000 tons, had 18-inch guns, and displayed the royal chrysanthemum on the bow. He placed his carriers several hundred miles in front of what he designated his main fleet, confidently planning to use them to clear the beaches for the invasion force and to draw out the American fleet for him to finish off with his big guns. His leading pilot, Commander Mitsuo Fuchida, commented wryly after the war that at Midway, "The officers and men of the big battlewagons were still confident that their massive firepower would win the [war-ending] battle when it came."[1] Yamamoto's death after his defeat at Midway seemed almost designed finally to teach him the superior force of modern air power. In 1943, while on an aerial tour of his Solomon Island command, his plane was shot down by American fighters alerted to his schedule by the code breakers in their Pearl Harbor basement who had set up his fall at Midway.

In time nuclear submarines armed with atomic missiles would displace the aircraft carrier as the world's first-line capital ship. But in the 1920s the aircraft carrier was still considered an auxiliary to the main line of battleships, and the champions of air power, the visionaries of the Japanese and American navies, had to fight to design and construct them. The two countries competed directly with each other under conditions imposed by the Washington Naval Treaty of 1922, which attempted to limit the major naval powers of the world by setting a 5–5–3 tonnage ratio for the British, American, and Japanese navies. The Japanese, with growing imperial plans, were embittered by being treated as a lesser power and at once began to rearm for the "big battle" they anticipated with the Yankee enemy, building new battleships and big carriers like *Akagi* (Red Castle) and *Kaga* (Increased Joy).

At the outset the Japanese, though advised by the British, who were leaders in carrier construction, were as uncertain as the Americans about the best design for their carriers and modified them constantly as they learned what worked and didn't work. As first built, for example, "*Akagi* had three separated, vertically arranged flight decks: an upper landing deck 190 meters (624 feet) in length, a middle takeoff deck for fighters 18 meters (960 feet) long, and a 49-meter (160 foot) deck beneath that for launching torpedo bombers."[2]

Like the American carriers *Lexington* and *Saratoga*, *Akagi* and *Kaga* were built on unfinished hulls of battle cruisers that, had they been completed, would have exceeded allowed tonnage under the Washington Naval Treaty. Commissioned in 1927, *Akagi,* the Japanese carrier flagship, was loaded with features that suggested its origin as a battle cruiser. It was a big carrier, 36,000 tons to begin with, and later modifications brought its displacement up to just over 41,000 tons. It was 855 feet long, and 102 feet wide after modifications, and had that distinctive Japanese open look under the flight deck at either end. Its decks could carry 63 planes, while 131,000 horsepower drove its four shafts and moved the huge ship at 31.5 knots. A peacetime crew of twelve hundred, plus eight hundred air personnel, manned the ship. Six guns of 8-inch caliber were in casemates below the flight deck, twelve 4.7-inch anti-aircraft and fourteen twin 25mm along the deck. The Japanese flight decks had 45mm wooden planks and 7mm steel plates. *Akagi* was armored with 10 inches of steel in a side belt, with a 3-inch armored deck above the machinery.

Kaga, commissioned in 1928, was patterned closely on *Akagi.* Originally it, too, had two hangar decks and a long, open bow plus turrets for 8-inch guns. The upper hangar deck was later closed in the same way as *Akagi,* and its guns were moved to stern casemates to allow extension of hangar and flight decks near the bow. It had a small island on the starboard side, and a trunk along the starboard side conveyed boiler gases aft.

Hiryu (Flying Dragon) and *Soryu* (Deep Blue Ocean Dragon), the other Japanese Midway carriers, were designed as carriers from the keel up and, though slightly smaller, re-sembled the *Yorktown* class of American carriers.

Commissioned between 1937 and 1941, *Yorktown* (CV-5 — carrier/heavier than air/number 5), *Enterprise* (CV-6), and *Hornet* (CV-8) were the American carriers that would fight the Battle of Midway. They reflected the time in which they were built. When the naval budget in a time of deep depression could not pay for the new American carriers needed to stay even with the Japanese, and when many workers were unemployed, *Yorktown* and *Enterprise* were built with money provided by the National Industrial Recovery Act to provide jobs for those out of work.

Many of the sailors aboard the ships were also there, as I was, because there were few jobs in depression America. The ships belonged to their time in other ways as well. Together with their planes the carriers represented an ongoing development of the Industrial Revolution from massive machinery and brute applications of energy to more sophisticated technology. From coal to oil, from steam to electricity and hydraulics, from mechanics to electronics, from two operational dimensions to three. The *Lexington,* the oldest of the first-line American carriers, with its huge General Electric turbo-electric drive was able to provide power needed by Tacoma, Washington, for a month in 1929 when that city's electric plant went down.

Within the American navy this technological shift was fought out in a running war beginning in the 1920s that did not end even with Pearl Harbor over the design of the new aircraft carriers. The old battleship "gun club" and the younger air-power enthusiasts, the "Airedales," known respectively, for their footgear, as the "Black Shoe" and the "Brown Shoe" navies, slugged it out. The first American carriers built after the Great War, *Lexington* (CV-2) and *Saratoga* (CV-3), were huge ships built on top of the hulls of heavy surface warships. They retained many gun-club features such as heavy armor and 8-inch surface gun turrets on the flight deck. They were designed to fight it out with any cruisers that might attack them when they formed part of a battle line or provided scouting for the main force of warships, which the old-line admirals considered their primary function.

The *Yorktown* carriers were, however, designed from the keel up as carriers and embodied many of the ideas of naval aviators who saw aircraft and their carriers as an attack force in their own right, capable of operating independently of surface battleships. They were smaller than the earlier carriers, making it possible to build more under the Washington Treaty limits. Tremendous fights in the Bureau of Ships marked the design phase of these new-style carriers. Arguments raged about the thickness of the armor belt below the waterline, of whether the carriers should carry heavy guns to defend themselves, of whether the flight deck should be steel or wood. At one point in the design phase the *Yorktown* had a flight deck that ended short of the bow to allow room for a forward gun deck with 8-inch turrets. Underwater torpedo tubes appeared in one carrier design but never got to the construction stage.

What the aviators wanted above all was speed in their ships and enough deck space to fly off their planes and land them safely and quickly. Speed to go into attacks and to get out again, speed to help launch planes by running into the wind, speedy movement of the planes on deck to get maximum strikes into the air quickly. Speed was the desideratum, and the aviators got it in the *Yorktown* class, that varied in details but roughly conformed to a pattern. The flight deck was 800 feet long and 83 feet wide, broadened slightly opposite the island to make for easier plane handling when the amidships elevator, one of three, was operating. Not fully loaded they weighed about 20,000 tons and drew 26 feet of water. Nine boiler rooms fed geared steam turbines driving four shafts and moving the ships in trials at 32 or

33 knots. They were a few knots slower when loaded for combat and their bottoms were fouled. Running at an economical speed of 15 knots they had a range of 12,000 miles, but at high speed they burned fuel at a far faster rate and in combat conditions needed to refuel every few days. A crew of twelve hundred was needed to run them in peacetime, considerably more, up to three thousand, in war when all battle stations had to be manned.

Mostly the Brown Shoes got their design right, but at times they bungled. Early designs had arresting wires forward as well as aft so that planes could be landed while the ship was reversing, since it was first thought that, depending on the wind, the carriers were as likely to launch and land planes while going backward as forward. Good idea, but it didn't work that way in practice. They also at first had transverse catapults forward on the hangar deck so that planes could be launched through the open side curtains while air operations were proceeding independently on the flight deck. Both these features were removed in later refits.

Guns? On this the Brown Shoes were definite. Guns weighed a lot, and so those aboard the *Yorktowns* were all for protection against air attacks, nothing really for surface defense. They were right; only once during the war, at Leyte Gulf, did Japanese gunners get several escort carriers in their sights, and aircraft soon drove them off. Eight 5″/38 anti-aircraft guns were located in four sponsons at the corners of the flight deck; four quads of 1.1s (later Bofors 40mm) were fore and aft of the island on

Fig. I USS *Hornet* launches a B-25 bomber during the Doolittle Raid, official U.S. Navy photograph 80-G-41197, National Archives, reprinted with thanks

the flight deck; and twenty-four machine guns lined the flight-deck catwalks, .50-caliber Brownings at first but later upgraded to 20mm Oerlikons. The number of guns and their placement were improved throughout the war, but they were never as effective against air attack as the fighter planes of the Combat Air Patrol directed by radar.

The main armament of the *Yorktown* carriers consisted of the seventy-two planes of an air group, though it was found that in the pressure of wartime operations eighty or more could be handled efficiently. The mix was constantly changing, but at the time of Pearl Harbor an American carrier air group was made up of four squadrons: a torpedo squadron, a fighter squadron, and two dive-bomber squadrons, one designated scouting and the other bombing. The bombing and scouting squadrons used the same plane, the Douglas SBD Dauntless, and both squadrons became dive-bombers for offensive purposes. That one squadron was designated for scouting, however, indicates the navy's continuing emphasis on the importance of scouting. In contrast, the Japanese concentrated on attacking aboard their carriers and left scouting to the floatplanes on their escort vessels. At Midway the destruction of the Japanese carriers can be traced to a scouting failure, while the Americans depended on land-based planes from Midway for the critical scouting reports.[3]

Optimally there were eighteen planes in each squadron, with a number of spares secured in the overhead of the hangar deck. After the war began it was clear that more fighters were required to provide both the combat air patrols needed to protect the ships from enemy planes and the escorts needed to accompany the dive and torpedo bombers on their attack. So the fighter squadrons got bigger. But the mix was considered critical, and the all-out coordinated strike on enemy ships that the navy aimed for was designed to distract the target with dive-bombers protected by fighters above while the torpedo planes, also protected by fighters, came in on the surface to deliver the knockout blow. In view of what would happen at Midway it is worthwhile to note that pilots recognized early on how difficult it was to coordinate such an attack, calling it a "Group Grope."

The art of handling the aircraft efficiently was developed by long practice and experience starting on the decks of the old *Langley.* The flight deck looked like a big war dance of different colors. The ordnance gang wore red cloth helmets strapped tight under the chin and a red T-shirt when they went about their work of loading machine guns, fusing bombs, and hoisting torpedoes on cables to secure them to the bomb racks. Other specialties wore different colors. Brown for the plane captains — one attached to each plane and responsible for its safety at all times that it was not airborne — green for the hydraulic men who manned the arresting gear and the catapults, yellow for the landing signal officer (LSO) and deck control people, purple for the oil and gas kings: it was all very colorful as we swirled around, moving smartly, getting the planes in the right places, ready to go. Everything was "on the double" and took place with whirling propellers everywhere, waiting to mangle the unwary. Crews of plane pushers in blue helmets and T-shirts, ran, not walked, back and forth, in the days before there were deck tractors, pushing the planes on deck forward to allow those in the air to land. And when the landing was complete, the planes forward were pushed back at a dead run to the stern so that they could be refueled and rearmed, readied to take off again. Planes needing work, engine repairs for example, were pushed onto one of the three huge elevators located forward, amidships, and aft. The elevator warning horn would blow, sounding like the automobile horns of the 1930s, GA-OOGAH, and a huge hole would open in the flight deck, lowering a plane to the hangar deck below, where metal curtains could be lowered at night and work go on under the lights while maintaining the blackout that the ship operated under from dusk to dawn.

Deck spotting was if not a science then a fine art on an American carrier, making sure that the planes were in the right place to take off quickly, that planes returning could land before their gas was exhausted, all without having to clear the flight deck. Timing and speed were crucial, and the Japanese would lose at Midway in part because of failure to manage their flight decks efficiently. They had opted early along to keep flight decks clear for landing and takeoff, stowing all other planes on hangar decks. This limited the number of aircraft, sixty-three on the *Akagi,* to the number that could be parked on the hangar decks, twenty-one Zero fighters, twenty-one dive-bombers, and twenty-one Kate torpedo planes. They were caught by our planes at the critical moment when they were unable to launch a strike against the American fleet, whose presence they had just discovered, because their flight decks were tied up launching and landing fighters to defend against attacking American torpedo planes.

By the time war came at Pearl Harbor, the Brown Shoe navy had the ships it wanted and had worked out ways to manage them and their aircraft effectively. When the ironclads could no longer provide the battle line, the aircraft carriers were there and ready to take their place. But the fate of these proud and seemingly invulnerable ships was built into them, not to become apparent until the Battle of Midway and the loss of the *Yorktown*. Armor and the location of the boilers were to be the critical matters.

Much of the weight of a warship, and its protection, are in its armor plating. The Washington treaty limited the weight of warships, which meant less armor or fewer ships. The Brown Shoes wanted as little armor as possible on their carriers in order to maximize the number built and increase their speed and range. They would have liked to do without armor altogether, but in the end they were forced to accept a compromise. The *Yorktowns* had light 2.5-to-4-inch armor belts below the waterline and an armored deck of 1.5 inches just above the vital machinery spaces and the magazines, considerably less than the thickness of armor built into a warship designed for gunfighting. Wooden flight decks weighed less than steel, and the supports rising from the hangar deck could be lighter as well, so wood it was, though the British had showed its value in the Mediterranean. Lighter armor made the *Yorktown*s fast, above 30 knots in trials, but it also made them, it turned out, vulnerable to damage by torpedoes. In the first year of the war, two of the three *Yorktown* class carriers were sunk by torpedoes. The USS *Yorktown* took two aerial torpedo hits and was abandoned, dead in the water, after a second attack on it at Midway. Reboarded, it was sunk a few days later by submarine torpedoes while under tow. The *Wasp,* similar in many ways to the *Yorktown*s, but smaller and even more vulnerable, was sunk by submarine torpedoes near Guadalcanal. The *Hornet* canted sharply to starboard, water on its hangar deck, from aerial torpedo hits at Santa Cruz in October 26, 1942. It was later sunk by Japanese destroyer torpedoes after it refused to go down under a barrage of 5-inch gunfire from American destroyers. *Enterprise* alone of this class of ship survived to become the most famous warship of World War II. It was hit many times by bombs but never by a torpedo. The official report on the sinking of the *Hornet* makes clear that the light armor plating in these ships had made them vulnerable to torpedoes:

At the time of the design of this class of aircraft carrier, naval treaties imposed a limitation on size which forced some sacrifices in torpedo protection, as compared with battleships, in order to gain other characteristics desired by the Department. The transverse depth of the torpedo protection system was considerably less than is now considered necessary for protection against modern torpedoes. Exact evaluation of the protection afforded by any given system is only possible by means of full scale tests in which the weight of the charge is accurately known. In the absence of such tests, extrapolations from 1/2 scale or smaller model tests is necessary, with considerable doubt, in our present state of knowledge as to the scale factor. All of the information available to the Bureau, however, indicates that this system should have withstood a charge of about 500 pounds of T.N.T. The indication, therefore, is that the particular Jap torpedo used in this case carried a larger charge, or a more powerful explosive, or both. Torpedo "E" is believed to have struck and detonated on the 4-inch special treatment steel side armor about two feet above the bottom of the plate. This conclusion is based on the location of the rupture in the holding bulkhead as reported by an eyewitness. If this location is correct, the armor belt apparently did not have any very great effect in reducing the damage from the explosion.[4]

The thinness of the armor plating in this class of ships was, with unforeseen consequences, linked to another design flaw. The ideal flight deck would have had no obstructions on it anywhere so that planes could be moved, landed, and launched without impediment. But a ship needed a bridge, as elevated as possible, and a flight control location, so there was always a need for some kind of an island structure on the flight deck. But what should be its size and location, port or starboard, fore or aft? The Japanese designers had the same problem and never settled on a pattern, building small island structures of different sizes in various locations. At one point in their design one carrier's bridge was even in the bow, just below the level of the flight deck. The American navy, however, settled on large starboard-amidships island structures, containing the bridge, the mast, and a single huge stack aft. With a large single stack available directly above, all nine boiler rooms were then collected amidships, venting directly upward through the island stack, thus avoiding space-devouring trunks running through the ship, heating up hard-to-cool areas below deck. On some Japanese carriers boiler gases were vented through a trunk flared downward, just below the flight deck, starboard amidships, on other ships through a long horizontal stack running from amidships to the stern, just outside and below the flight deck.

The *Yorktown* design seemed practical, but it violated the usual navy arrangement of alternating boilers and machinery rooms to prevent all or most of the boilers and the steam power from being knocked out by a single torpedo or bomb hit. The *Yorktown* carriers, it emerged at Midway, with all boilers concentrated in one area, could go dead in the water with a hit, from either bombs or torpedoes, while the rest of the propulsion machinery might be still functional. This is exactly what happened to the *Yorktown* at Midway: "Aside from personnel casualties, the most serious effect of this bomb hit was that it ruptured the uptakes from boilers 1, 2, and 3, completely disabled boilers 2 and 3, and extinguished fires in boilers 2, 3, 4, 5, and 6. The fire rooms containing all saturated boilers (1, 2, 3, 4, 5, and 6) were filled with smoke and gases from the bomb hit and from the boilers themselves."[5]

A carrier that cannot move at high speeds while under air attack is a sitting duck, and this is exactly what happened in all

Yorktown class losses.[6] Captain Charles Perry Mason of the *Hornet* in his action report after his ship was sunk later in the year was brief and explicit about what a single torpedo could do to these big ships: "The key ship of a task force must not be completely disabled by one torpedo."[7]

THREE

Obsolete "Devastators" and
Obsolescent "Wildcats"

The American navy talked at the outbreak of the war as if its aircraft were the best in the world, but this confidence, insofar as it was real and not just bluster, was possible only because so little was known about the Japanese planes we would soon be fighting. The Japanese had been demonstrating the quality of their aircraft in China for a number of years, but just how little we knew is there in the surprise of a naval pilot training as a carrier pilot in San Diego when he heard that the Japanese had attacked Pearl Harbor. If anyone should have known what the Japanese had in the way of planes, it should have been a carrier pilot who had just been through pilot training and was on his way to the Pacific Fleet. But on the day of Pearl Harbor Fred Mears was startled to discover that he and his fellow pilots were totally ignorant of what they would shortly be facing: "Suddenly we realized that nobody knew anything about the Japs. We never had heard of a Zero then. What was the caliber of Jap planes and airmen? What was the strength of the Japanese Navy?

What kind of battles would be fought and where? Apparently we were woefully unprepared, lacking planes and ships, and the Japs had struck hard. They had caught us in the landing circle with our flaps down. As if waking from a long sleep, we slowly became aware of facts that we hadn't thought about before."[1]

The Battle of the Coral Sea, just before Midway, had shocked the American navy with what it revealed about both our planes and those of our enemy. Our fighter planes were inferior to the Japanese Zero, and our torpedo plane was obsolete. Only one of our carrier planes stood out: the SBD Dauntless dive-bomber made by Douglas was the top of its line. Only these planes in the carrier air group had enough fuel to deal with the delays imposed by carrier warfare, still hit the enemy hard, and then return to their ships. The SBD-3 was in service by the first half of 1941 and much praised by its pilots for its durability and flying qualities. With a 1,000-horsepower Wright Cyclone engine, it could fly 250 miles an hour and carry a 500- or a 1,000-pound bomb under the belly, plus 100-pounders under the wings. The Dauntless carried two men, pilot and radioman/gunner, with two synchronized .50-caliber machine guns firing forward through the propeller and two .30-caliber free machine guns on a ring in the radioman's cockpit. With a loaded weight of slightly over 5 tons it could reach 27,000 feet and had a range of about 1,300 miles. These are optimal figures, of course, provided by the makers from carefully controlled tests, and in service few if any planes ever achieved their builder's ratings, but the Dauntless could stay in the air for long periods. When Lieutenant Commander C. Wade McClusky led the *Enterprise* dive-bombers far past the point where the Japanese fleet had turned north, he had enough gas to conduct a search that eventually led him to his targets and brought him home, though with less than 5 gallons in his tank.

The other carrier planes in service at Midway were less well adapted to their functions. The fate of the American torpedo planes at Midway was closely linked to the failure of the Grumman F4F Wildcat shipboard fighter to handle its opponent, the Japanese Zero fighter. The F4F-4 model was a midwing metal monoplane with manual retractable landing gear and backward-folding wings for carrier stowage. It had a wingspan of 38 feet, a length of 28 feet, 9 inches, a wing area of 260 square feet, and weighed 5,785 pounds when empty and 7,975 pounds when loaded for combat. The Wildcat had a power plant of a 1,200-horsepower Pratt and Whitney R-1830-86 double-row radial engine, which gave it a maximum speed of 320 mph at 19,800 feet. With this weight and its small wing surface, it had a wide turning radius and a slow climb rate, critical matters in combat with the very maneuverable Zero. The F4F-4 model had six .50-caliber machine guns in the wings, but could carry only twenty seconds of ammunition for each gun. The earlier model F4F-3 had only four guns and fixed wings, but it was generally preferred because it could carry more ammunition per gun and with less weight could stay in the air longer. The Wildcat was stubby in design, looking like a bee or, as someone put it less politely, a flying beer bottle. It guzzled gas at high rpm when

Fig. 2 Grumman F4F "Wildcat" fighter, official U.S. Navy photograph NH 97493, National Archives, reprinted with thanks

climbing to high altitude, and its stated range of 845 miles was very optimistic. By the time it took off, circled for a bit to join up with other planes, and then flew 100 or so miles to an attack, it had only about a half-hour of combat at full military power before it had to return to its carrier. But the Wildcat was rugged and would get home even when shot to pieces. The famous Thach Weave maneuver, developed by Lieutenant Commander John "Jimmy" Thach, made the best use of the Wildcat's heavy armament and its sturdy construction in air combat, but the Weave was a defensive, not an offensive, formation. The plane had been in development since 1940 and was the Grumman Aircraft Engineering Corporation's effort to produce a naval fighter plane that could hold its own with any in the world. The Wildcat did not, but Grumman would soon produce its successor, the famous F6F Hellcat, which entered service in 1943 and controlled the Pacific skies, along with the Vought F4U Corsair, for the remainder of the war.

The Japanese Zero fighter was our nemesis. The Mitsubishi A6M fighter, or Zeke as we called it, was the most famous of the Japanese military aircraft, and at the Battle of Midway, where the ships' antiaircraft fire was comparatively ineffective, Zeke ruled the air, shooting down most of the American torpedo planes before they could get in range to drop their torpedoes. The Zero entered service in 1940, and by the time of Pearl Harbor, its expert, highly trained pilots had developed formidable fighter tactics. Modified throughout the war, the A6M2 was the version that fought at Midway so effectively. It had a 950-horsepower Nakajima radial engine, and with a wingspan of 39 feet, it weighed just 3 tons. As in all the Japanese carrier aircraft, durability and safety were sacrificed to speed, maneuverability, and range. Pilots had no armor, and when hit heavily, Zeke, like all other Japanese planes, would usually burn because of light structural materials and the lack of self-sealing gas tank liners, but they were hard to hit.

The Zero was not only maneuverable, it was fast, with a top speed of 331 mph, and it could reach 16,000 feet in about six minutes and then go on up to 32,000 or 33,000 feet. At cruising speed with the frequently used auxiliary tank, Zeke had a maximum range of nearly 2,000 miles, even with heavy armament. Two 20mm cannon were in the wings, and there were two synchronized 7.7mm machine guns. The machine guns were used for ranging and the 20mms for knockout shooting. A graceful plane, the design of Japan's greatest aeronautical engineer, Jiro Horikoshi, the Zero is remembered as the equal of the other great fighter planes of World War II, the British Spitfire, the German Messerschmitt 109, and the American P-51 Mustang. But it turned out to be vulnerable to the rugged, fast Hellcat once that plane appeared in the Pacific in 1943.

Our fighters were at a disadvantage with their Japanese enemy, but the American torpedo plane was a real turkey. The TBD-1 (Torpedo Bomber, made by Douglas, Model 1), the Devastator, was the first all-metal carrier monoplane in the American fleet. It had been in service nearly five years when the war started, but it was already obsolescent, obsolete really, though we didn't know it, or maybe just hadn't admitted it yet. The TBD-1 carried a torpedo externally, slanted forward and downward, and had a takeoff weight of nearly 10,000 pounds. A 900-horsepower Twin Wasp radial engine gave it respectable numbers in the handbook, but in the fleet, the numbers dropped alarmingly. The problem was evident in the landing characteristics of the plane, which, when it approached stalling, lacked power to keep it from settling too rapidly. As a result, many pilots hit the ramp while landing on carriers. Worse still, loaded with a torpedo weighing over a ton, the old Devastator consumed between 30 and 50 gallons of fuel an hour, depending on its speed and its climb rate, but could carry only a reduced amount of its maximum 180 gallons of gas.[2] The problem of the reduced fuel in the tanks with a torpedo aboard cannot be overestimated, for it severely limited the pilot's ability to reach an enemy, make a combat run, and then get back to the ship. The problem was compounded when departure on a strike was delayed until the entire group was in the air and assembled. An unfavorable wind for launching burned up yet more gas. Such were the conditions on the *Hornet* at Midway, and Waldron, knowing that he did not have the gas to return to the ship, planned to go on to Midway, a shorter distance, after the attack.[3] On June 4, despite efforts to close on the Japanese fleet, the American carriers had to turn away from the Japanese so that they could launch and land planes in a light southeasterly breeze throughout the day.

Hinged wings folded over the TBD so that more of these planes could be accommodated on a carrier. The wings contained flotation bags, with a lift of 3,400 pounds, to keep the Devastator afloat and salvageable after water crashes, but the plane lacked self-sealing gas tanks, which made it vulnerable to fire at Midway. Carrying a crew of three — pilot, observer/bombardier, radioman/gunner — Devastators had one synchronized .30-caliber machine gun firing forward through the propeller and a .30-caliber machine gun on a scarf ring for use by the radioman in the rear seat. After the war began, this after machine gun was changed to a dual mount that had more firepower yet added more weight and was hard to handle in the slipstream. The landing gear was retractable hydraulically, but the lower half of the wheels still showed even when fully retracted, supposedly to help in emergency landings.

Loaded with bombs the TBD could use the Norden bombsight as a horizontal bomber. It was never very effective in this role, but the Norden was the prize American secret weapon of the time—"bombs in pickle barrels from 10 thousand feet" the U.S. Army Air Force bragged—and the navy wanted it, even if it had to put the Norden on a relatively small plane like the TBD. The mid-seat observer was also the bombardier, and when the TBD was used as a high-level bomber, the bombardier crawled down from his seat, lay flat under the pilot, and aimed the bombsight through a slanted forward window. Slow, with limited range, and lightly armed, the TBD's only plus was that it was extraordinarily stable, with a wingspan of 50 feet and a large wing surface of 422 square feet.

The navy knew the deficiencies of the Devastator, and a replacement, Grumman's TBF-1, became standard after Midway. A detached section of Torpedo Squadron Eight with six TBFs attacked the Japanese carriers from Midway Island, along with four army air force B-26 Marauder medium bombers modified to carry a torpedo. Grumman soon turned the dies to make the TBFs over to General Motors, and from that time on they were known as TBMs, fondly called "Muffies" by the thousands of young men who flew in them. But at Midway the TBF for all its increased power, speed, and armament fared no better than the

Fig. 3 TBD-1 "Devastator," 1938, official U.S. Navy photograph 80-G-9341, National Archives, reprinted with thanks

TBD, for five out of the six that participated were shot down by Zeroes, and the survivor was wrecked, its gunner dead and its radioman wounded and unconscious.

The Japanese torpedo bomber was much superior. The Nakajima B5N torpedo bomber, known to us for identification purposes as Kate, was the workhorse of the Japanese carrier forces from 1940 until it became obsolescent in 1944. More of these stripped-down planes were sometimes included in a Japanese carrier air group than any other type, and they justified the faith placed in them, putting three American aircraft carriers, *Lexing-*

ton, Yorktown, and *Hornet,* out of action with torpedoes in the
first year of the war. The B5N-2 had a 1,000-horsepower engine, weighed only 9,000 pounds loaded with a torpedo, and
had a wingspread of slightly over 50 feet, which was reduced
by half when the wings were folded overhead for storage on
board a carrier. Its wheels were fully retractable. A loaded 1,200-
mile range was optimally possible, as were speeds of 235 mph
and an altitude of 27,000 feet, though again these are builder's
numbers. Lightly gunned, with only one after machine gun, its
main weapon was the Japanese aerial torpedo, not the famous
Long Lance used on surface ships and submarines but Type 91,
Mod. 2, an oxygen-driven aerial torpedo, 18 feet long, with a
17.71-inch diameter, weighing 1,840 pounds. Kate could carry
bombs of similar weight and was often employed as a high-level
bomber, using an aiming device to attack from level flight. Kate
could be easily identified by the distinctive way it carried its torpedo or bomb, somewhat off-center to starboard, in order to
clear the sight line for a bombardier lying in the belly. American
sailors came to hate to see Kate, having likely flown long distances, come over the horizon, for Kate's pilots were extremely
skillful and courageous, resolutely pressing home their attacks
with their very trustworthy plane and powerful torpedo.

   Just how aircraft design can affect operations shows up clearly
in a contrast of the range of Japanese and American planes.
Range figures have to be cut in half to allow carrier planes to go
out to their target and then return to the carrier. So a 400-mile
range, which might sound good, meant point to point but for

carrier operations meant a maximum 200-mile strike radius, without a safety factor. Further, the handbook ranges for both American and Japanese planes were optimums, and in practice in the fleet, ranges measured either by distance or by hours of flying time were greatly reduced by the realities of carrier flying. A carrier plane spent some time on deck warming up and taxiing, burning gas all the time, before taking off at full power, gulping fuel. And once in the air it might circle for up to an hour getting into formation and waiting for other squadrons in the air group to get airborne and form up before departing for the concerted group attack that was doctrine in both navies. This meant in turn staying together and required flying in formation, which needed a lot of throttle jockeying to maintain position, burning even more gas. Full military power during combat, throttle to the firewall, turning up high rpm, swallowed gasoline by the barrel. Then you had to turn around and go back to the carrier, circle while waiting your turn before landing, and then fly a long, roundabout approach. Many carrier planes came back aboard with thimblefuls of gas in their tanks.

As a result of the limited range imposed by the realities of naval aviation and coordinated strike tactics, American carrier admirals preferred to launch an attack as close to the enemy as possible. At Midway, 155 miles was the distance between fleets at launch on June 4, and Admiral Spruance would have preferred a distance of 100 miles. On some occasions in the war, such as at the Coral Sea — 170 miles — and at the Battle of the Philippine

Sea, when the risk was thought worth it, the American commanders would go for longer distances, but when they did, not all the planes would make it back aboard.

Range dramatically affected the fate of both the American torpedo planes and the performance of the fighters at Midway. On the morning of June 4 at approximately 0600, when the American commander, Admiral Fletcher, knew for sure that the Japanese had been sighted, he ordered Spruance to begin moving west to close on the Japanese and launch the critical first strike as soon as they were definitely located. Fletcher may have intended locating the enemy and launching the strike to be simultaneous—the wording is ambiguous: "Proceed southwesterly and attack enemy carriers as soon as definitely located. I will follow"—but Spruance, not an aviator, chose, on the advice of his air staff, to close the enemy to lessen the distance for the attack even after he had their exact location shortly after 0600. Distance was approximately 200 miles at that point. He launched everything available at about 0700, estimating the distance to the Japanese at 155 miles, hoping to catch the Japanese with their pants down. He was right, and his torpedo squadrons began to arrive, one after the other, just as the Japanese were recovering the last planes that had attacked Midway and were trying to ready their first strike against the newly discovered American fleet. A longer delay could have cost us either the battle or, which would have come to the same thing, our carriers. If the American aircraft, however, had been able to launch at 200 miles, as the Japanese could and did, Spruance would have gained a crucial half hour on his enemies before they were aware of the American presence.

Throughout the day limited range affected our planes, particularly the fighters. Grumman Wildcats had about half the range of the Dauntless dive-bombers, and in the ten-plane Fighting Eight detachment from the *Hornet,* every plane ran out of gas and landed in the sea without ever sighting the enemy. The fighters from the *Enterprise,* Fighting Squadron Six, circled above the Japanese fleet for a time but left the scene of the battle without engaging the enemy because they were short of gas. Six Wildcats from Fighting Squadron Three off the *Yorktown* gave Torpedo Squadron Three the only fighter protection afforded torpedo planes that day, but they broke off after mixing it up with the Zeroes and losing a plane. When Jimmy Thach called for the survivors of this group to rendezvous, Ensign (later Commander) Tom Cheek was unable to go to the rally point 20 miles north because "to get there would take fuel that I did not have to spare."[4]

With their lighter planes and bigger fuel tanks, plus auxiliary drop tanks on the Zeroes—which our planes did not have at Midway—the Japanese were much less limited in the distance at which they could launch strikes. Zero fighters based in Formosa (Taiwan) at the beginning of the war were able to fly to Luzon, fight there, and return to their home fields. At 0430 on June 4, the Japanese launched their strike on Midway Island at 200 miles. At 0859 the last of them landed back on their ships, the fighters having engaged in combat along the way, the bombers having attacked the Midway defenses. Their scouts, except for an older plane with low fuel capacity from a battleship, were able at the end of a 300-mile vector out to make a 60-mile dogleg flight and then return 300 miles or more to their home ships. Some were able at Midway to remain over the American fleet for a good part of the day, sending crucial reports back to their carriers.

Design differences were not the results of chance or fashion but reflected differing national attitudes toward war and the value of individual life. Where we chose ruggedness and safety for the flyers, to put it simply, the Japanese opted for performance and distance, sacrificing crew safety and endurance to achieve these goals. No design details are more telling in this regard than the absence in Japanese planes of armor behind the pilot and of self-sealing gas tanks.

In contrast, American pilots and aircrews loved our planes for the armor that protected them, the self-sealing tanks, and the way the planes' rugged construction would bring you home even after heavy damage. But the price paid for valuing life over performance was that our planes at the beginning of the war were outclassed by their Japanese opponents, which could fly much faster and farther. Later in the war more powerful engines made it possible to build faster American planes without sacrificing their safety features, but at the time of Midway our planes were not as fast or maneuverable as the Japanese, and their range was comparatively limited by their weight and fuel capacity.

FOUR

Duds: The Great American Torpedo Scandal

Navies were very high on torpedo planes as ship killers at the time of the Midway battle. At Taranto on November 11, 1940, the British, flying an obsolescent, very slow biplane, the Fairey Swordfish, known as "the stringbag," went into a harbor in the south of Italy at night and crippled the Italian fleet, flying straight and level to within 700 feet of the targets. They repeated their success at the sinking in the open Atlantic of the German super battleship *Bismarck* in May 1941, when, flying in unbelievably bad weather, they put a torpedo into it that locked its steering gear and forced it to steam in circles, making it an easy prey for the warships that then came up and sank it with gunfire. The great aerial torpedo attack of all time, however, was the Japanese assault at Pearl Harbor. Japan sent in forty planes carrying torpedoes and got nineteen hits and nineteen explosions. The targets were, of course, tied up and unprepared for an attack, but the number of hits was still very impressive, especially in water that was shallower than optimal.

For all the reputation torpedoes had, the American versions had many problems. The Mark 13 aerial torpedo dated from the early 1930s. It was stubby, 13 feet, 5 inches long and 22.4 inches in diameter, and heavy, weighing 2,216 pounds. Its warhead originally contained 400 pounds of TNT, later 600 pounds of Torpex, which gave it more bang but made it nose-heavy. Its speed was 33 knots, with a short range. Like most torpedoes at that time, it was a self-contained, small steam-propelled submarine. The warhead, with a built-in exploder, was mounted forward of an air flask filled with compressed air that forced alcohol—which is where some lucky old salts got their shipboard alky—and water together in a combustion chamber to make the steam that drove the turbine and the propulsion system. The tail had the control fins and two propellers controlling torque by turning in opposite directions. Gyroscopes and guidance mechanisms were in the after section to control depth and direction.

Much that was wrong with the American torpedo delivery system was widely known before the war, but "despite remaining problems, in the spring of 1941 officialdom pronounced the Mk 13 an 'all-up round' with estimates of 80 per cent reliability when dropped from 140 ft [altitude]. The ordnance bureau's assessment proved absurd. Fleet squadrons, which knew better, limited drop parameters to a maximum 110 knots at 50 ft or less, severely limiting torpedo tactics."[1] One history says that the torpedoes had twelve major defects and remarks, "It is hardly an exaggeration to say that the performance of the Mark 13 was so bad (until finally improved in 1944) as to make American torpedo-plane attacks well nigh futile."[2]

The problems grew with the training, or lack thereof, of the pilots to drop torpedoes. When George Gay, the sole survivor of Torpedo Squadron Eight, went up on the deck of the *Hornet* on June 4, 1942, to get into his TBD and fly off to attack the Japanese fleet, he had never flown a plane with a torpedo on board, let alone dropped one. He, in fact, had never even seen a plane with a torpedo take off from a carrier: "Well, Torpedo 8 had a difficult problem, we had old planes and we were new in the organization. We had a dual job of not only training a squadron of boot ensigns, of which I was one of course, we also had to fight the war at the same time, and when we finally got up to the Battle of Midway it was the first time I had ever carried a torpedo on an aircraft and it was the first time I had ever taken a torpedo off of a ship, had never even seen it done. None of the other Ensigns in the squadron had either."[3] The pilots of Torpedo 8 had flown two or three torpedo-drop training flights a month, to judge from the flight log of another young squadron pilot, Ensign Grant Teats, but neither real nor dummy torpedoes were carried on these practice runs. The drops were simulated with smoke bombs marking the point of release.

Torpedo 8 was a new squadron, with many barely trained new pilots and radio/gunners who knew Morse but had no gunnery instruction. The squadron had been formed in the summer of 1941 to go on board the *Hornet* when it was commissioned later in the year. But old hands in torpedo planes didn't have a lot more experience, and perhaps even less trust in their weapon:

> Simulated torpedo runs were seldom carried out other than during Fleet problems or local maneuvers. Once a year each pilot was to make a live drop, with a dummy head on a real torpedo. There was no practice scheduled using cement logs such as evolved later. We made no drops in 1939. In 1940 we made two dry runs on a regular target towed by a mine sweeper or tug, then the big day, taking off from North Island with a Mk 13 hanging out of the bomb-bay! On the first live drop . . . the "fish" dropped clean. It ran true for the first 100–150 yards, then veered 60 degrees to port and took off over the surface like a happy trout. . . . From the "scuttlebutt" going the rounds at Pearl, ours was not an isolated incident with torpedo drops. All the available evidence is that the Bureau of Ordnance and Bureau of Aeronautics had more than adequate warning as to what was going to sea as torpedo armament.[4]

There was a chronic torpedo supply shortage that had its roots, as so many navy dispositions did, in turf and politics. The single prewar naval torpedo factory at Newport, Rhode Island, on Goat Island in Narragansett Bay, was an old-fashioned facility where a lot of the parts were made slowly, and not always interchangeably, by hand. This factory fiercely defended its monopoly and, supported by the Rhode Island congressional group, reacted angrily to any criticism. As a result we went into the war with a handcraft method of producing torpedoes and an inadequate supply of them that was not remedied until after a second factory was reopened later in the war in Alexandria, Virginia — still against the fierce opposition of Goat Island. The chronic shortage that resulted from this situation was what gave torpedo plane pilots such rare chances to practice with a torpedo.

Then too, torpedoes were so expensive, about ten thousand dollars apiece, that a navy with an annual budget of around three hundred and fifty million dollars in the Depression years of the 1930s practiced with them very infrequently and then only with the greatest care lest they be damaged or lost. Even the old hands in the air groups and on the subs had never made a war shot. "When World War II began there was no one in the Navy who had ever seen, or heard, a torpedo detonate."[5] Those who flew at Midway were not surprisingly unsure of just what they had done or should do while trying to hit a Japanese carrier at Midway with a torpedo. Here is a gunner's description of the confusion about the crucial issue in his plane: "I was not aware or did not feel the torpedo drop, probably because Corl [the pilot] was turning and trying to jinx [sic] a little bit. A few days later I asked him when he dropped. He said that when he realized that we seemed to be the only TBD still flying and that we didn't have a chance of carrying the torpedo to normal drop distance, he dropped at greater than normal range. At about this time probably, I couldn't figure out what he was trying to do

Fig. 4 Douglas TBD-1 "Devastator" drops a Mark 13 torpedo, Official U.S. Navy photograph 80-G-19229, National Archives, reprinted with thanks

and the flak was really bad; so I yelled into the intercom, 'Let's get the hell out of here!' It is possible that my yell helped him make his decision."[6]

Gay knew so little about his weapon that he couldn't even properly identify the kind of torpedo he had under his plane: "We had torpedo planes, but we had to use old submarine torpedoes." It wasn't as bad as that, the torpedo squadrons were using the standard American aerial torpedo, the Mark 13, but experience with it after the war began added to the general feeling of nervousness about the weapon. The famous Jimmy Thach told of watching in crystal-clear water our torpedoes in an early attack in New Guinea run under their targets only to explode spontaneously on the other side or bury themselves in a mud bank. At Tulagi on May 3, 1942, twenty-two torpedo planes got just one hit against very light opposition. Things looked better a few days later, on May 6, when some six or seven torpedoes from *Lexington* and *Yorktown* planes were reported to have hit the light carrier *Shoho*.[7] But two days after that in an attack on the big fleet carrier *Shokaku,* twenty-one Devastators from the *Lexington* and *Yorktown* launched twenty torpedoes, and all missed. "The Japanese noted that the torpedoes had been launched from too far out and that they ran so slowly in the water as to be easily avoidable."[8] They were also avoidable because, using air for pressure, they gave off a track of hydrogen bubbles that revealed their path. American aviators on this strike blamed the failure on the slow speed of the TBD—which surely ought to have been no surprise to them by that time—

and erratic behavior by their torpedoes. But the Japanese, who at this point in the war were openly contemptuous of the Americans and their equipment, were right.[9] The main troubles were with pilots who nervously dropped too soon torpedoes that ran too slowly. Lieutenant (jg) Robert E. Laub, one of the few survivors of Torpedo 6 at Midway, spelled out the consequences of the slow speed of the Mark 13:

> To have a reasonable chance of obtaining a hit on a ship capable of making 25–30 knots with our present aircraft torpedo, the point of dropping must be at a target angle no greater than 70° on either bow end at a range of approximately 800 yards. The reason for this statement is obvious when the fact that our aircraft torpedo has a maximum speed of 33.5 plus or minus .5 knots is considered. Any drop which the attacking [attacked?] ship can cause to be a "Trailing Shot" has practically no chance hitting the target due to the respective speeds. In other words, the torpedo will probably never reach the target before it runs out and stops. At high speeds, the leads necessary are so large that even at 800 yards range a slight misjudging of the target's speed or lead to be given will result in a miss. High speed targets are the only targets discussed because in a task force containing carriers no attacks will be made on any other ships except the carriers, while one is still afloat, and all carriers are capable of a 25–30 knot speed.[10]

Given the deficiencies of the American torpedoes, a day of terrible failure was sooner or later inevitable. It came at Midway. With not a single explosion, the few torpedoes that were dropped there before the planes were shot down were as ineffective as George Gay and his fellow pilots had heard and believed before they lugged them out to the Japanese fleet: "We had built and installed what we called 'Stater Vanes.' . . . This was a big plywood bomb tail that we hoped would give the thing some aerodynamic characteristics and enable it to enter the water without going end over end. I don't know whether mine went in right, ran true and got a hit, or whether it went straight to the bottom. It may have turned around and gone back to Pearl Harbor for all I know. What I know for sure is that I tried. The Japanese torpedoes were almost exactly twice as good as ours were at this time. They could drop them twice as high and fast and then count on them running almost twice as fast."[11]

Gay was mostly right about the Japanese aerial torpedo, which weighed less, 1,840 pounds, but carried 610 of explosive in the warhead. Its other advantages over the American Mark 13 were its speed, 42 knots, and range, 2,400 yards, and the crucial fact that it could be dropped while the carrying aircraft was going a maximum of 260 knots. Our navy thought that the Mark 13's sensitivity dictated that it be dropped with the utmost care, eased into the water as gently as possible to avoid disturbing its delicate innards. This unexamined theory generated near-suicidal dropping practices. The only chance you had of putting one home, it was believed, was, as the skipper of Torpedo 8, John Waldron, instructed his boys, to get inside 800 yards, fly very low, 100 feet or less, and very slow, 80–100 knots, very straight and level, and very close to the target, releasing at an angle of no more than 70 degrees. This both made you a sitting duck for shipboard antiaircraft firing point blank and gave any fighters sharking about plenty of time to put you down. But these killer delivery tactics were standard operating procedure. The old Indian, John Waldron, knew what flying this pattern took, and he told his boys what it was. "If worst comes to worst and we find ourselves alone and outnumbered by the enemy planes on the way into the attack, we'll keep boring in toward the carrier. If there is only one man left I want that man to take his pickle in and get a hit."[12]

Early in the war torpedo research as well as production was still in the hands of the Goat Island people, who thought they had already designed and made the perfect aerial torpedo, and no tests were run to explore just what did happen to a torpedo when dropped from a plane at various speeds and altitudes. Later work in scientific labs at Caltech and elsewhere showed, however, that the slow, flat drop the torpedo pilots died executing was the surest way to mess up a torpedo's directional and depth controls, causing the fish to run erratically. The best height from which to drop aerial torpedoes was, it was discovered, something around 800 feet and at a speed of over 200 miles an hour. This allowed the fish to enter the water vertically rather than horizontally, and this kind of entry was in fact found to be less jarring to the sensitive internal mechanisms than the belly flop of the standard delivery technique. The men at Midway would have given themselves and their torpedoes a better chance if they had roared in at 500 feet with "balls to the wall," let the torpedoes drop nose down, and gotten the hell out of there.

Naval air was not the only service having difficulty with torpedoes at this time. A great torpedo scandal that pitted the Pacific submarine force against the Bureau of Ordnance and the Goat Island torpedo makers raged during the first years of the war over the problems with the American torpedo. The shortage showed up early when subs in Pearl Harbor preparing to go on war patrol in the far Pacific had to transfer any unfired torpedoes to their own tubes from subs returning from a patrol. Older torpedoes built in the early twentieth century were dragged out of "obsolete and obsolescent" storage to fill in during the great torpedo shortage of 1941 and 1942. The destruction of a store of two hundred torpedoes by Japanese planes at Cavite in the Philippines crippled the Asiatic fleet destroyers and submarines.

The submariners, who had had little more prewar experience with firing live torpedoes than the naval air people, discovered soon after the war began that their standard Mark 14 torpedoes, which were larger and faster but internally very similar to the Mark 13 aerial torpedo, were extremely unreliable. They detonated early, they ran deeper than their settings, they porpoised and circled, and when they hit the target, they often did not explode. The kinds of problems that drove the submariners wild were played out in one of the war god's many ironies at Midway. An American submarine picket line had been set up before the battle, but it was located in an arc beginning southwest of Midway and was out of position to intercept the Japanese carriers coming in from the northwest. However, on the morning of June 4 the *Nautilus,* at the northeast end of our submarine line, was spotted by the Japanese and between 0700 and 1000 was depth-charged and strafed. Somehow it survived, and later in the day it had worked itself into a position where it could fire three torpedoes at a Japanese carrier burning from the dive-bombing attack earlier. *Nautilus* reported that it had sunk the *Soryu,*[13] and the major American history of submarine warfare in the Pacific contains a bold drawing of a torpedo blasting the Japanese carrier and sending it to the bottom: "*Nautilus* Sinks *Soryu.*"[14] But the carrier was actually *Kaga,* and far from sinking it, *Nautilus* provided some of its crew with a lifeboat: "Two of the torpedoes barely missed the ship, and the third, though it struck, miraculously [*sic*] failed to explode. Instead, it glanced off the side and broke into two sections, the warhead sinking into the depths while the buoyant after section remained floating nearby. Several of *Kaga*'s crew, who were swimming about in the water after having jumped or been blown overboard when the bombs struck the carrier, grabbed onto the floating section and used it as a support while awaiting rescue. Thus did a weapon of death become instead a life-saver in one of the curious twists of war."[15]

And so it went everywhere in the submarines. The *Tunny* outside Truk fired ten torpedoes at a sitting duck that brought not a single explosion. Perhaps the biggest scandal was a sequence of events that "culminated on 11 June [1943] in a string of failures by our submarines in Tokyo Bay to sink any fleet units, although *Trigger*'s skipper reported explosions after a full salvo successfully fired at carrier *Hiyo*."[16]

Despite frustrations of this kind, it took a long time and a lot of near-insubordination before the submariners forced the Bureau of Ordnance to accept that several things were wrong with the torpedo itself. The Mark 14, it was finally officially admitted, ran on average 10 feet deeper than its setting, and the Mark 6 magnetic exploder in the warhead, which was thought to be one of the big secrets of the war, was likely to explode prematurely or not at all. When the submariners refused to use it any longer, against direct BuOrd commands, and fell back on the backup mechanical exploder, it, too, often failed. The striker would jam in its rails at any angle but failed most often in a head-on zero-degree hit, supposedly the ideal hit.

There was no aerial torpedo war with BuOrd. The aviators grumbled but seemed to accept their fate, though the Mark 13 had the same problems as the Mark 14. The magnetic exploder was not, however, one of them, since the Mark 13 still used the Mark 4 mechanical exploder, and it was a bit more reliable at the slow speed of the Mark 13 torpedo because, ironically, it hit with less inertial force than the faster Mark 14 and therefore did not jam as frequently. But duds were still frequent, and the aerial torpedoes shared all the depth-setting problems and the tendency to run erratically.

A Mod. 2 aerial torpedo, an improved version with the 600-pound Torpex warhead, which threw its balance out of whack, was capable of 40 knots, which at least solved the speed problem. When it reached the fleet just after Midway, Bureau of Ordnance instructions allowed it to be dropped at speeds up to 200 knots and at altitudes from 235 to 365 feet, the latter considered a maximum for emergencies only. But later that year at the Battle of Santa Cruz, with the new TBFs and presumably the Mod. 2 torpedoes, everything still went wrong.

> Six *Hornet* planes tried to launch torpedoes at the heavy cruiser *Suzuya*. One hung up and failed to release, two ran erratically, and although the crews claimed to see the other three explode, one on the starboard side and two on the port side of *Suzuya,* these sightings either were products of youthful imagination or prematures triggered by the tricky Mark 6 magnetic exploder. The exploder often would activate the warhead just short of a ship's hull and result in a toss-up of water that gave every appearance of being a hit. The five *Enterprise* torpedo planes also attacked a ship they thought was a cruiser, but the ship's only damage came from a vicious strafing attack delivered simultaneously by Jimmy Flatley and his flight of Wildcats.[17]

From that point on the Pacific Fleet was very chary in its use of aerial torpedoes. The Mark 13 remained, however, the American aerial torpedo until the Korean War, when it was used to destroy dams in North Korea. But improvements to the Mark 13 began to get results in 1943 with:

> a pair of wooden girdles. One was a drag ring—they called it the "pickle barrel"—a plywood sleeve snugged over the torpedo's head. It slowed the air-flight speed by nearly 40 percent, reduced in-air oscillations, even acted as a shock absorber when the torpedo struck the water and broke off. The other addition was a shroud ring—pilots called it a "ring tail"—that fit over the aft end. It added stability in the water like feathers on an arrow, and suppressed hooks, broaches, and underwater rolls as well. With these two major additions (and the strengthening and repositioning of inside components), the Mark-13 completed an almost miraculous transformation: straight and true runs began approaching nearly 100 percent. The eventual result of the early theoretical studies, the Cal Tech development, and the Fort Lauderdale deepwater testing was a Mark-13 that could be launched at altitudes up to 800 feet instead of the conventional 50 feet, and at air speeds as high as 300 knots—a change that resulted in a 40 percent hit rate, and much less stressed pilots.[18]

But all this was long after the torpedo pilots at Midway had flown their suicidal drop patterns with fifty-one untrustworthy torpedoes, getting not a single explosion on a Japanese hull.

FIVE

Indians and "Ringknockers": Personnel of the Midway Torpedo Squadrons

During the course of the war carrier squadrons were whittled down mainly to pilots and aircrew. Maintenance and repair personnel became a permanent part of a naval air station or a carrier. But the Midway squadrons still had all the needed service people attached. Mechanics, ordnance men, instrument technicians, radiomen, parachute riggers, metalsmiths, master-at-arms, you name it, a squadron had at least one. At any given time there were up to several hundred men in a squadron, and when the squadron moved it was a big deal, something like a gypsy caravan with huge amounts of equipment, boxes of tools, baggage by the carload, spare parts for the planes.

The four squadrons that made up a carrier air group were assigned early in the war to a particular carrier. Air Group Six was on the *Enterprise* (CV-6), but "Airedales" and ship's company seldom mixed. We were transient and they were not. Whenever the ship was in port we were ashore with our planes, living in barracks, coming aboard only just before sailing.

The full-service squadron was a cumbersome but a clubby arrangement. On board ship the enlisted men filled up a big compartment with bunks four high in the after part of the ship, where dirty gray salt water sloshed across the deck of the head as the ship rolled back and forth, and small aluminum lockers lined the bulkheads to hold all a sailor's possessions. Each trade had a shop where it hung out, kept its tools, brewed coffee, and shot the shit. The radiomen/gunners that flew in the rear seats — a chief or first-class aviation radioman usually flew with the commanding officer — were privileged as flight personnel to hang out in the squadron office or the back of the ready room. These were the aristocrats of the squadron's enlisted men.

The ordnance shack on the *Enterprise* was on the gallery deck just under the flight deck, next to the stack, and to reach it from below you had to go up a long ladder the height of the hangar deck and then down a corridor with wire cages on either side. This was very difficult at General Quarters when, with alarms ringing and bugles blowing, we tried to make our way up the ladder while large numbers of other sailors whose stations were somewhere near the golden rivet that was said to be at the bottom of the ship tried to make their way down. The torpedo squadron ordnance gang occupied two cages, one on either side of the corridor, the first for storage and heavy work such as belting ammunition, the other for standard repairs. Homer Murphy, the ordnance chief, and Freddy Moyle, the first-class ordnance man, held forth near the coffeepot, keeping an eye on the rest of us. The coffeepot was old and had three blue hash marks for major overhauls, plus a red "E" for efficiency with three stripes. Here Murph mixed his "moose milk," coffee laced with bombsight alcohol, scorning the less pure torpedo alky that had to be refined to be drinkable. Murph was an old Arkansas razorback, mildly drunk most of the time and endlessly amiable. No one ever had a more agreeable boss, though he couldn't pronounce "aluminum," of which we used a lot, in the usual way. "Get some of those lum-lum screws and change the bomb racks on Tare 7," was the best he could do. His standard advice when he watched us awkwardly making a difficult repair was, "If you can't fix it, get a bigger hammer."

In the early days of the war almost all enlisted men were from blue-collar, lower- or lower-middle-class homes. We would have denied that we were an underclass, there wasn't such a thing in America we thought, conveniently forgetting that blacks and Asians were allowed to serve in the navy only as officers' cooks and mess attendants. Our teeth were terrible from Depression neglect, we had not always graduated from high school, none had gone to college, our complexions tended to acne, and we were for the most part foul-mouthed, and drunkenly rowdy when on liberty. We certainly didn't look like heroes. With no understanding of social class, I used to wonder in the shower or the crowded compartment when everyone was dressing why so many of us were skinny, bepimpled, sallow, short, and hairy. We bragged, however, about what we would do when we got liberty in Honolulu again, about the cars we had driven and the girls we had known in civilian life. You had to wonder some-

Fig. 5 Paul Cadmus, *The Fleet's In,* 1934, oil on canvas, National Archives, Navy Art Collection, Number 34-005, reprinted with thanks

times why any of us had joined the navy, so good were the lives we described at home. In truth we were a very ordinary group of young men, some new recruits, others petty officers with years of service and training behind them, all volunteers, all regular navy, USN, many planning to learn a trade and spend twenty to thirty years in the navy and then retire on a small pension. We talked not of politics, and "flag-waving" was scorned, something for officers giving us pep talks and civilians far away from combat. We were patriots only in the standard American assumption that our country was the best in the world.

The officers called us by our last names and we called them "Sir." Few enlisted men knew an officer as a person, which meant that the deaths of the pilots when they came were not felt very personally. We felt them as fans feel the loss of a game by their football team. There was always a lot of tension between the enlisted men and the officers, largely based on the enlisted men's real fear of officers, who looked down on them, and the officers' reciprocal fear that their orders would not be obeyed by men they never quite trusted. Naval caste squared with social class. The pilots were not themselves from very high on the social ladder but were mostly middle-class young men. A few old regular navy who had graduated from the Naval Academy led the squadrons and filled their crucial positions like XO and flight officer. Of the fourteen pilots who flew at Midway in Torpedo Squadron Six, nine were USN, an unusually high number, but most of the flyers at Midway were young ensigns and lieutenants (jg), college, not academy, graduates, who had gone through a crash program to train reserve aviators designated AV(N). There were also a number of enlisted pilots, naval aviation pilots (NAPs), who held the rating of aviation pilot just as other enlisted men were torpedo men or aviation mechanics. Some of them had been promoted to warrant officers after the war began and, if young enough not to look too salty, were made ensigns and junior-grade lieutenants. It is perhaps worth noting that the enlisted or former enlisted pilots on the carriers had a very high survival rate at Midway, four out of the total eight torpedo squadron survivors. One can only speculate that they had had a lot of flying time and had learned to nurse their old planes and limit their gas consumption.

Whatever their backgrounds, all officers at least early in the war had a godlike status that was spelled out in a popular novel of the time, one of those flimsy paperback war editions, Marcus

Goodrich's *Delilah* (1941). These books were handed out free at the ship's library. They were of an odd size that could be stowed in your hip pocket and read in odd corners of quiet by the few readers aboard ship. This one was about an old coal-burning destroyer in the Philippines before World War I and was popular not only because it told a fine adventure story but because it paid a lot of attention to what was really the navy caste system, spelling it out better than any of us could have, but in a way that we accepted as totally accurate:

> Between the Commissioned Officers and the crew, the limits and barriers, like foundations that grow broader and vaster as they sink deeper into the earth, become less matters for understanding than for apprehending, and intangible though they are, their formidable cleavage makes of the group in the Wardroom a different order of beings from the group in the Forecastle. To the enlisted men, amongst whose various grades of Chief Petty Officer, Petty Officer, Seaman and Fireman the rigid limits and barriers are not set up, the Commissioned Officers loom as a kind of golden, incomprehensible cloud ever on their horizons, a removed, privileged existence almost beyond aspiration, beyond envy, a cloud to be understood, as an entity, only through portents, signs, visitations and, in a measure, through long experience, an aureate nimbus from which the inescapable lightning plays, supervising every detail of their existence.[1]

It was up to the officers to live up to this image, and some of them made an art of it. Lieutenant Commander Eugene Lindsey, the stern, young commanding officer of Torpedo 6, landed awkwardly on the way to Midway, not quite getting all the plane aboard when he cut the throttle. The big plane bounced up in the air and descended, half on the deck, half hanging over the port side, across the catwalk, before sliding into the ocean. Lindsey should not have been flying—he had concealed eye trouble —but he was determined not to miss the great battle. So he was hauled back on board and taped from the navel to the armpits for a badly wrenched back, his face so badly bruised that he could not bear to put his goggles down. Yet when it was suggested that he stay in sick bay on the day of the attack, he replied, "This is what I have been trained to do," and led his squadron into the greatest sea battle of the century, where he and most of his men died.

Appearance was a big part of caste distinction. Aboard *Delilah*, the destroyer's sailors were always black with coal dust from shoveling fuel into the boiler and greasy from rusting machinery. There was no coal on board the *Enterprise*, but the men were always wet with sweat and frequently dirty from the hard work most of us regularly performed. Cosmolene used to fight rust seemed designed to smear a pair of clean dungarees with stains nearly impossible to remove. Gone were the crisp, bright-white shorts and T-shirts of peacetime, even white socks and white hats were forbidden lest they twinkle in the distance and betray the presence of the ship to a snooper. Everything we wore

was dyed a sickly blue that faded to something even worse without a name in the color chart. Laundry was done in a huge bag
for an entire division at the same time, and when it came back,
unironed of course, and was dumped in a big pile on the deck
in the division's compartment, we would sort through looking
for the blue dungarees and work shirts stenciled with our names
across the back in black ink. Anything fresh we put on was soon
soaked with sweat anyway, so wrinkles didn't matter.

Officers seldom dressed in their white or blue uniforms at
sea, at least in the tropics. Khaki was the uniform of the day,
but the laundry managed to make officers look starched and
clean compared to the crew. A sartorial ensign from the pages
of *Delilah* would have caused no surprise if he had come down
the long ladder from the flight deck of the *Enterprise,* past the
torpedo shop and around the dark hole of the 'midships elevator: "He had managed, as always . . . to change into an immacu-
late uniform . . . tinted a delicate coffee brown . . . brass buttons
were highly polished and the gold shoulder straps glistened. His
shoes were shined and his cap sat on his carefully combed hair
at a precise and interesting angle."[2]

Commissioned pilots were, like the cast favored in the war
movies of the time—a street-smart kid from Brooklyn, a slow-
talking farmer from Kansas, a rich and pampered boy from
Princeton—a mixture of America at the end of a long depression. We hooted at these Hollywood clichés when there was a
movie in port on the hangar deck, but the squadron officers
fitted the pattern. "Moose" Moore was an academy graduate,

quiet and easygoing, speaking only in a shy way. Kelly was a champion lacrosse player from Maryland, Evans was a Harvard law student from Indianapolis who was known as "Squire" because of the tweed jackets and gray flannels in his locker. Another pilot, "Whitey" Moore, looked like Dagwood, the comic strip character, and was a frenetic jitterbugger who could "fall asleep on a picket fence." He was also the pet of his squadron, and his commanding officer was particularly concerned for him, getting quite annoyed when other pilots painted a moustache on him while he was sleeping. "Plywood" Teats from Oregon would not allow his name to be pronounced "Tits," and considered every order as interference in his personal life. He got his "moniker" from an impromptu lecture he gave on making plywood, a business he had been in before the war. "Abbie" Abercrombie hailed from Kansas City and was a pessimist who presciently called Torpedo 8 the "Coffin Squadron," believing that torpedo planes were a catastrophe waiting to happen. He always wanted to know how far something was from Kansas City. Threatening to request a transfer always, he never did, and one can imagine his thoughts as he rode his old TBD into the ocean at Midway. There were others, all familiar types, the drugstore cowboy, the uxorious newly married man, the joker, none of whom, except for Abercrombie, seemed to be very worried about the dangers of their line of work. George Gay, the only survivor of the *Hornet* torpedo planes at Midway, had a reputation in his squadron for being a Texas loudmouth.[3]

The outstanding aviator on board for the Midway battle was

Lieutenant William "Gus" Widhelm, USN. One of his squadron mates describes him in a memorable way:

> I considered LCDR Gus Widhelm, the XO of VS-8, to be the best combat flight leader in the *Hornet* air group. I have often wondered what might have happened if he had been CHAG [commander *Hornet* air group, pronounced Sea Hag] at the BOM [Battle of Midway]. Gus was combat fearless and a superior naval aviator. On the morning of June 6th, the third day of the BOM, Gus was the flight leader of the morning attack on two cruisers and some destroyers. Gus briefed the flight in the VS-8 ready room and told us he was going to drive a bomb down the stack of the biggest cruiser. As we approached the targets, Gus broke loose from our formation and did a solo dive on a cruiser and "nailed" it just aft of the stack. Now that was leadership! I know every pilot in that flight wanted to show Gus we could also get a direct hit. We tried, but our results were poor due to lack of experience diving the SBD. Gus was an avid crap shooter and poker player who would bet on anything. He won a bet on a golf course that he could hit a ball farther with his putter than his golfing buddies. He won! Gus was once asked by some reporters if he ever got scared flying combat. Gus told them that he bragged so much he had to live up to his words! He was killed in Texas about twenty years after the war, showing off by attempting to do a low altitude slow roll.[4]

There was a writer in Torpedo 8, an observant man named Frederick Mears, new to the squadron, who didn't go on the Midway attack but was killed the next year "in the line of duty" on a raid at Rekata Bay, Santa Isabel, in the Solomon Islands. Before he died he wrote a fine book that deserves to be much better known than it is, *Carrier Combat,* in which he tells us a great deal about his squadron and its rough-and-ready skipper.

Lieutenant Commander John Charles Waldron, skipper of Torpedo 8, was an intriguing man. His place in the history of American arms — Davy Crockett at the Alamo and George Armstrong Custer come to mind — has been much neglected. From a more populist background than was usual for a naval officer in the 1920s, he was born in Fort Pierre, South Dakota, on August 21, 1900. The youngest child of five in a Catholic family with Oglala Sioux blood (genes nowadays) on the mother's side,[5] he moved with them at an early age to the small village of Lashburn, Saskatchewan, where the family grew vegetables, which the boys sold to the Indians in the winter, touring about on a sled. He apparently got tired of eating dried fish while staying with Indian hosts, for his daughter recalls, "I remember my father never wanted any sea food of any kind."[6] On a Naval Academy form he described his father's business as "farming and stock raising," and a relative remembers the man as "a dealer in horses, a mean man, and cruel."[7] His cruelty may, of course, have been just the hardness required to break horses.

"Johnny," as he was known in military service, came back from Canada, quarreling with his father, to go to high school in Rapid City, South Dakota. His mother taught in an Indian school, and a strong belief in education ran through the family. Having difficulty getting into Annapolis, he went to a cram school, Ferris Institute at Big Rapids, Michigan. Appointed by his congressman in 1920, he struggled with his studies at the academy and was known as a "boner," what we would call a "grind," hitting the books long and hard. His academy record gives him high marks in "executive aptitude" but low ones in ordnance and gunnery. He got forty-three of sixty points in navigation, however, a course of considerable interest in view of what would happen at Midway. He was right to be concerned about his studies, for in 1924 he graduated 479 out of 525. Not much of an athlete either, clumsy apparently in the manner of country boys who never played on athletic teams, he finally settled for wrestling and boxing, without much success. His daughter Nancy says he "had to give it [sports] up due to repeated injuries." He was diagnosed with tuberculosis in his last year of studies, but there is no description of treatment, which must have been quick and successful. Or maybe the diagnosis was premature. At any rate there was no interruption in his career.

After graduating Waldron served on the cruiser *Seattle* and in 1926 went to flight school in Pensacola, Florida, where he earned his gold wings in 1927. He and Abigail Wentworth, daughter of a Pensacola attorney, married in 1929 and had two daughters, Nancy and Anne. As his widow she returned to Pensacola. To judge by one story, they must have drunk as heavily as many Americans in the 1920s and 1930s: "One family joke about

Johnny and Abigail, is that the morning after an evening at the Officer's Club Johnny told her she'd done a good job of driving them home the night before, and she said, 'Me? I thought you drove home'!"[8] "He loved the navy, travel, parties, tennis and golf," says his daughter Nancy, and drove a fancy Lincoln Zephyr, which he was willing apparently to lend to his squadron members.

The Waldrons moved about a lot, like most naval officers, and Waldron acquired a reputation as inclined to be direct in his view of things and free in speaking his mind. But, everyone agreed, a great pilot. He studied law at some point and was admitted to the California bar, though apparently he never practiced. Going from one assignment to another, flying all types of aircraft in the 1920s and 1930s, he rose in rank to lieutenant commander by 1939, when he worked at the Bureau of Ordnance and was a naval observer at the Norden bombsight factory. Then in July 1941 he was given command of the new Torpedo Squadron Eight.

Waldron looked a bit like a Sioux, with a dark complexion and a hawkish face. Mears found him fascinating and observed him closely, painting a variety of word portraits that bring out a complex character. Under the lively professional naval officer there was another man whom Mears reveals in a series of sketches so quick that they leave us wondering what we saw: "After asking a question the Skipper had a characteristic way of leering out of the corner of his eyes at the squadron, his head cocked, his mouth open in a silly, almost idiotic, fashion. Suddenly he would snap his mouth shut like a trout after a fly, straighten his head, and begin to stroke his chin, staring at them from under his bushy eyebrows and beseeching the answer."[9] Mears is a master of the single word, "beseeching" in this case, that cuts to the center of his subject, revealing in a flash what is otherwise totally concealed.

Waldron would throw big busts for his boys after he had worked them fiendishly hard all week and get roaring drunk with them. He invented a squadron symbol, a clenched fist, and a war cry, "Attack." These must have been something of a joke to his green pilots, for on the way to attack the Japanese carriers at the Battle of Midway, two of them, Ensign Albert K. Earnest and Ensign Charles E. Brannon, the first survived the disaster but the second who did not, "across the tail of Feeb's [group leader Lieutenant Langdon K. Fieberling] plane exchanged their own version of the squadron's attack signal (arm extended with closed fist) by raising an arm closing the fist except for the second finger, the goosing finger."[10] But however funny it may have seemed to his juniors, when Waldron's emotional temperature was running high he would stand up, clench his fist, and shout "Attack," in the middle of parties or on any occasion, suitable or unsuitable. There was a manic streak in him, and on one morning, upset that things had not gone well the day before, he ran into the squadron Quonset hut in Hawaii where his boys were sleeping soundly and emptied his .45 caliber Colt automatic out the door shouting to them to get up and go to war. Which they did, in a hurry. All this was only a prelude to impulsive behavior, both lethal and heroic, as we shall see, during the attack on the Japanese at Midway.

There was also a reflective side to him that comes out in a letter he wrote to a nephew who was just entering pilot training. It is worth repeating in part, for it bears closely on the final moments of his life:

> Some day you'll be out there on the Pacific [Major Robert Philip, USMC, was killed there on June 24, 1943] or down around Haiti or Central America some place and you will be out all alone, and there won't be any gals to cheer you on, and you will just get in a hell of a fix. Your nerve alone won't pull you through, and you will find it a situation not described in any book and no one ever told you about it. The greatest factor which will prevail in pulling you out of a jam is to be able to call upon, instantaneously, something from a vast fund of knowledge of things aviation that have stacked up between your ears. I advise you to read the preceding paragraph over and over again. The ability to call upon a sort of sixth sense has pulled me out of a jam at least six times and saved my life. And it will do the same for you provided you take this business seriously. It is a serious business and it is not a sport.[11]

For all his oddities, his men really liked Waldron because he was concerned about them and dedicated to their deadly trade. He was a perfectionist and worked his raw beginners night and day trying to get them ready for the big battles to come. But, for reasons we have already seen, the training, through no fault of his, was hollow at the core, failing to provide practice taking off with or dropping either a dummy or a live torpedo. So he made his boys endlessly practice angles of attack and release, using a "mooring board" he devised, and if they followed his rules, he assured them, a well-planned and firmly executed attack could not fail to drive home several "fish." He never called a torpedo a "torpedo." It was always a tin fish, a pickle, a weenie, a tor-pecker, or "one of those goddamned things." Though his own experience was limited, he drilled his flyers on what the big targets, the Japanese carriers, were likely to do when they sighted the Devastators of Torpedo 8 bearing down on them: "I had learned from Commander Waldron in his lectures that ships, especially large ships of that kind [carriers] when they commit themselves to a turn, full rudder or something, it is quite some time even if they apply full reverse rudder, it will be some time before they are able to straighten down and usually he told us from reports and things the Japs would nearly always commit themselves when subject to torpedo attack, they will maneuver."[12] He taught them to use a torpedo director sight mounted in front of the pilot, which turned out to be useless, and he concentrated on making them learn by rote the standard, but near suicidal, dropping procedure. "Tex" Gay knew the lesson so well that he would repeat the rules when he was boring in on a Japanese carrier, the last man alive in his squadron: "I had been told that the ideal drop was 1,000 yards range, 80 knots speed, and 80 feet or so of altitude."[13]

Fig. 6 Aviation Chief Radioman Horace Dobbs (left) and his pilot. John Waldron, 1942, official U.S. Navy photograph 80-G-41187, National Archives, reprinted with thanks

Waldron taught his boys a lot more than torpedo tactics. He made them run around the flight deck to keep in shape, even though the other squadrons laughed at them and called them "boy scouts" or a "circus." He badgered them about their equipment, insisting that they carry knives, and forced them to make more comfortable and safer shoulder holsters than standard issue to carry their Colt .45 automatics, even providing some cow skin that he said was best for that purpose. He taught them, Gay remembered, that if they ever "got in a spot . . . never to throw anything away." This last might sound like a commonplace of living in the country where the store was a long ways away, but it saved Gay's life. When a cushion floated out of his crashed plane at Midway, he remembered what Waldron had said, saved it, and used it to hide under during a long day. Waldron also forced his boys to at least observe things officer-pilots usually knew nothing about, engine changes, loading bombs, the workings of their plane's hydraulic system. And despite constant instructions about this and that, the men of Torpedo 8 loved and respected the strange man who was to lead them into death. "Waldron commands the respect of every man in the squadron. He is lean and brown, with the keen eyes and firm mouth of the professional. He takes care of his men and is continually on the lookout for their welfare. He is well liked for his wry sense of humor. Most important of all, he has a gallant fighting spirit and knows his job thoroughly."[14] What professional could wish for a more perfect obituary than this, written by one soon-to-be-dead pilot, Mears, for his commander already dead in battle.

Waldron's image has a lot of dark areas, and some of his peers thought him more than a bit odd. No one had more doubts about him than Commander Stanhope Cotton Ring, a naval *beau ideal,* commander of the *Hornet* Air Group at the Battle of Midway, who would have a lot to do with the fate of Torpedo 8. If Waldron was a typical shaggy aviator, somewhat uncouth with no side about him, Ring belonged to the starchy, do-it-by-the-book side of the navy. He was what was known at the academy as a "ringknocker."[15] Waldron and Ring represent the extreme ends of the range of naval officers before the war, and the difference between their types had a lot to do with the way the ships were run and the war was fought.

Born in 1902, the son of a commodore in the old navy paymaster corps, Ring was appointed to the Naval Academy from the fourteenth district of Massachusetts, paying his required three hundred and fifty dollars for textbooks and uniforms in 1919. His grades were higher in executive abilities than in engineering subjects. At twenty he weighed 152 pounds, standing at six foot, two inches, and was inevitably called "Slim." With a bland face, he was considered exceptionally handsome and a ladies' man, a "horrible snake" in the Annapolis slang of the time. Never missed a hop. According to the 1923 yearbook, *The Lucky Bag,* he was cool, content to let his studies take care of themselves. He played a lot of bridge on summer cruises, hiding out in lifeboats or in the bag locker. He must have been bright enough to get by, since he graduated fairly high in his class, 87 of 414.

He served first on the battleship *Colorado* and went on to a wide variety of assignments. He won his navy wings in 1927, the same year as Waldron—they must have known one another at Pensacola—and flew off our first big aircraft carrier, the *Lexington.* He served on an admiral's staff and later became naval aide to President Herbert Hoover. He married Eleanor Reynolds, and the couple had three children. For a time he ran the administrative division of the Bureau of Aeronautics in Washington, D.C., and when war began in Europe he went to London as assistant naval attaché at the embassy and then served as an observer on a British aircraft carrier in the Mediterranean, learning what radar, which the United States did not have at the time, could do for carrier operations. The British made him a commander, Order of the British Empire.

He was not deskbound all his career by any means. He helped develop navy dive-bombing and became a member of the "Caterpillar Club," survivors of a parachute jump, when his bomber caught fire in an air show and he had to "hit the silk." He credited his gloves with saving his hands and is said to have introduced the shipboard ritual of holding up your hands to show you are gloved when taking off from a carrier. The fire left a faint imprint of his goggles on his face, adding to his distinction. He was handsome and charismatic, popular with women and easy with his superiors, who liked him and saw that he got the right jobs.

Before the *Hornet* was commissioned Ring got the plum assignment of its air group commander, but his command didn't go particularly well and ended with disaster at Midway. A martinet, he was not a successful leader. Getting ready to sail to battle at Midway, for example, he confined everyone in his squadrons to their station, standing regular watches, while the pilots from the other carriers were partying on the beach at the Royal Hawaiian Hotel. After this, "The *Hornet* squadrons were not exactly a band of brothers."[16] Long periods spent in administrative positions had left him not as skilled as a pilot and an air group commander as he should have been. His wingman at Midway has a telling story of their first meeting on the hanger deck of the

Hornet in Norfolk harbor: "I noticed an SBC-4, with 'CHAG' painted on the side, tied down on the hanger deck. At the time I didn't know this was the group commander's aircraft. The biplane's landing gear was damaged, its 'flying wires' supporting the wings were broken, and the wings were drooping. I never heard an explanation, but I assumed that CHAG had wanted to make the first carrier landing on the *Hornet*. It must have been a lulu! You had to work at making a bad landing in the SBC-4!"[17] Interestingly in view of what was to happen, Ring's navigation was shaky. During the *Hornet*'s shakedown cruise he got lost in the Gulf of Mexico and Gus Widhelm had to take over and lead the air group back to the ship. The pilots of the *Hornet* Air Group blamed him for their failure to find and attack the enemy carriers at Midway. Before this flight was finished every one of his four squadrons had without permission left him to try to return to the ship. Ring was, however, awarded a Navy Cross for his service at Midway, the same decoration that Waldron received.[18] But in 1946, as we shall see, he was still trying to explain in a never published handwritten letter his actions in a way that cleared him of blame. He hid the letter away in a chest in his closet, and it came to light only many years after his death.

Despite his failures at Midway, Ring commanded carriers later in the war, and his last ship was the old *Saratoga,* which he delivered to Bikini Atoll as a target for atomic bombs in 1946. He would, everyone knew from the start, end an admiral, maybe even the chief of naval operations, but he didn't reach this rung. A "tombstone promotion" to vice admiral when he retired was his high-water mark. Before he retired in 1955 he was the administrator of the Marshall Islands and ended his career as the commander of the joint Mediterranean fleet. He died in San Diego in 1963.

Waldron and Ring were the "hairy" and the "smooth" types of the naval officer corps that commanded the U.S. Navy at the beginning of the war. The tensions between these types were written into the history of the Pacific war, leading to a major disaster at Midway and other places like Guadalcanal.

SIX

Attack: "My God, This Is Just Like Watching a Movie"

The Japanese decision to attack Midway and occupy the island was firm by the end of April 1942, and orders were cut to the various units involved early in May. The Japanese spy system no longer functioned in Hawaii, so there was no information that the American carriers and their escorting cruisers and destroyers had left Pearl at about the same time that the Japanese fleets were sallying. Their intelligence told them, quite wrongly, that the remaining American carriers were still in the Coral Sea guarding the route to Australia and that the *Yorktown,* like the *Lexington,* was either sunk or so badly damaged as to be incapable of battle. For the attack they laid elaborate plans requiring coordination of six fleets:

- The invasion fleet of troop transports from Saipan
- A covering fleet from Saipan for the invasion fleet
- Admiral Nagumo's attack fleet of carriers and escorts, *Kido Butai,* charged with smashing Midway defenses before the invasion

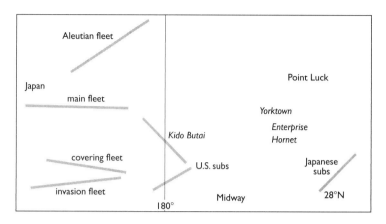

Fig. 7 Disposition of the fleets on the morning of June 4, line drawing by author

- The main fleet of Admiral Yamamoto and his battle line, masked behind the attack fleet
- An Aleutian fleet to take Attu and Kiska
- A submarine fleet posted northwest of Oahu, between Pearl Harbor and Midway

The Japanese invasion fleet was spotted by Midway scouting planes on the morning of June 3, and it was attacked by army B-17s and then by patrol planes from Midway without much success. The B-17s were one of the big disappointments at Midway, as they had been earlier in the Philippines. Touted as America's super weapon, as many Flying Fortresses were crammed onto Midway as could be parked in the limited areas bordering the runways. Bombing from high altitudes, they disrupted Japanese fleet formations, but they got no hits at Midway. Four PBY Catalinas made torpedo attacks against the invasion fleet more than 400 miles southwest of Midway on the night of June 3–4.[1] Torpedoes were not the weapons of choice for these big, long-range patrol planes, but the pilots and crews were game to try. The Catalinas tracked the foe in the moonlight, and three of the four managed to launch at ships. One explosion took place, "in itself rather remarkable for an American torpedo of that period," on a small tanker, but the ship did not lose place in the formation.[2] The hit sounds doubtful, but it went into the American navy books as a hit, and the Japanese recorded an attack and hit of some kind on the *Akebono Maru,* which makes it the only American torpedo explosion against a Japanese hull in the Midway battle.

The attack may have had negligible effect, but the discovery of the Japanese ships told the Americans for certain that the Hawaiian code center's intelligence had been accurate and that the battle was on. The Japanese remained untroubled by the discovery of their invasion transports by land-based planes and proceeded toward their objective confident that there were no American carriers in the neighborhood. By that time, however, the *Yorktown* (Task Force Seventeen), and *Enterprise* and *Hornet* (Task Force Sixteen), under the overall command of Admiral Frank Jack Fletcher on a speedily repaired *Yorktown,* were past the Japanese submarine line established too late between Oahu and Midway and had proceeded west and south of Point Luck, the hopeful name of their rendezvous, to about 200 miles northeast of the Japanese attack carriers and about 300 miles north-northeast of Midway. The American strategy was an ambush, lying unobserved off to the east to launch full-load strikes from all three carriers, when *Kido Butai*'s position was established by Catalina scouts from Midway.

The plan was cool and simple, but the minds of those who had to execute it, particularly in the torpedo squadrons, where the men had some inkling of what a desperate mission they were scheduled to fly, were not: "We didn't get much sleep the night of June the 3rd, the stories of the battle were coming in, midnight torpedo attack by the PBY's, and all kinds of things, and we were a little bit nervous, kind of, like before a football game. We knew that the Japs were trying to come in and take something away from us and we also knew that we were at a disadvantage because we had old aircraft and could not climb the altitude with the dive bombers or fighters and we expected to be on our own. We didn't expect to run into the trouble that we found of course, but we knew that if we had any trouble we'd probably have to fight our way out of it ourselves."[3]

As the night wore on George Gay and the other pilots tried to sleep, but they were up before two o'clock to grab a cup of coffee and sit nervously in their ready rooms waiting for more information on the Japanese fleet they now knew was for sure out there. Everyone was nervous. Waldron told his boys that this was the big battle they had all been waiting for: "It will be a historical and, I hope, a glorious event."[4] To his wife in the letter Waldron wrote that morning he was more open in his doubts: "You know Adelaide, in this business of the torpedo attack, I acknowledge we must have a break. I believe that I have the experience and enough Sioux in me to profit by and recognize the break when it comes — and it will come."[5] Marc Mitscher, the captain of the *Hornet,* later reported that Waldron knew "that there was the possibility that his squadron was doomed to destruction with no chance whatever of returning safely to the carrier."[6] Nor was Waldron alone in his premonitions. Various sources speak of censored letters from people who were killed filled with more than usual forebodings.

Reveille also came early on the *Yorktown* on June 4, 1942, a day of spotty visibility and light winds from the southeast. The ship's pilots and aircrew had earlier been told in an intelligence briefing that "if only three TBDs out of your fifteen plane squadron survive the run-in to deliver torpedoes, you will have accomplished your mission."[7] The numbers were just about right. Only two planes of Torpedo Squadron Three made it back from the attack, and both had to land in the water near the carriers.

At 0430, Thursday, June 4, Nagumo's carriers on a heading of 130 degrees launched an attack with half of their planes on Midway, 200 miles distant, and as a precautionary measure began sending out scout planes on 300-mile searches east and northeast to look for any American warships that might just possibly, but not likely, be lying out there. As a precaution, however, the planes remaining on board the four carriers were loaded for attack on ships — that is, with torpedoes and armor-piercing bombs — should any be discovered. No one could fault the Japanese to this point. They were playing a strong hand skillfully.

At 0530 a Midway patrol plane sighted a single Japanese carrier, which was enough for the Americans to confirm that the Hypo intelligence was totally accurate. And a 0552 patrol plane report of "two carriers and main body of ships" told our carriers that this was their primary target. At 0553 another message reported that a large group of Japanese planes had been sighted heading toward Midway. It was now clear that the Japanese fleet had committed itself to attacking the island and must therefore still be ignorant of American naval presence on its flank. At 0603 another message gave more information on the enemy fleet's size and location: "Two carriers and battleships bearing 320 [from Midway], distance 180, course 135, speed 25."

On Midway, when told that the PBY scouts had spotted the Japanese carrier fleet, the six TBFs of the detached and upgraded Torpedo 8 section started their engines and taxied out to the runway.[8] They were followed by four army B-26s also carrying torpedoes, which had been modified and sent out from Hawaii in the all-out effort to hit the Japanese with anything that could get to them. The planes flew out together into an orange sky at 0615 on a heading of 320 degrees. It was then that Ensigns Earnest and Brannon exchanged their own version of Torpedo 8's attack sign. Ten minutes into their flight they were attacked by two fighters from the incoming Japanese strike, which they identified as Messerschmitts. Unlikely, if not entirely impossible, but aircraft and ship identification in the excitement of battle were often irrational, as this was, and often wrong. But there had been scuttlebutt that the Germans were helping the

Japanese. This was first combat for these crews, and there was a holiday atmosphere in the air. They sobered up when they looked back and saw planes burning in the air over Midway, and then proceeded on their way under the clouds about 4,000 feet up toward the Japanese carriers. At 0710 they attacked. Commander Fuchida, a senior flight leader, who was recovering from an emergency appendicitis operation, managed to get up to the deck of the *Akagi* to watch the course of the air versus ship battle:

At 0705 a bugle sounded, "Air raid!" and all eyes in the flight command post turned toward the southern sky. I managed to pull myself up for a look and noticed that it had become a beautiful day. There was fairly heavy cloud cover at about 6000 feet, but the air was clear and visibility good.

A destroyer in the van section of our ring formation suddenly hoisted a flag signal, "Enemy planes in sight!" Emitting a cloud of black smoke to underline the warning, she opened fire with her anti-aircraft guns. Soon we spotted four planes approaching from 20 degrees to port. They looked like torpedo bombers, but before they could get close enough to permit confirmation, our fighters had pounced upon them and shot down three, causing loud cheers all around me. The last plane gave up the attack and withdrew with our Zeros in hot pursuit.

A bridge-top lookout was heard from a moment later:

"Six medium land-based planes approaching, 20 degrees to starboard. On the horizon." Scanning the sky to starboard, sure enough, I saw the enemy planes flying in a single column. It looked as if the enemy had planned a converging attack from both flanks, but fortunately for us the timing was off.

Following the lead destroyers, our cruisers opened fire. Then battleship *Kirishima,* to starboard of *Akagi,* loosed its main batteries at the attackers. Still they kept coming in, flying low over the water. Black bursts of anti-aircraft fire blossomed all around them, but none of the raiders went down. As *Akagi*'s guns commenced firing, three Zeros braved our own anti-aircraft barrage and dove down on the Americans. In a moment's time three of the enemy were set aflame and splashed into the water, raising tall columns of smoke. The remaining three planes kept bravely on and finally released their torpedoes. Free of their cargo, the attacking planes swung sharply to the right and away, except for the lead plane which skimmed straight over *Akagi,* from starboard to port, nearly grazing the bridge. The white star on the fuselage of the plane, a B-26, was plainly visible. Immediately after clearing our ship, it burst into flames and plunged into the sea. About this time several torpedoes passed to port of *Akagi,* trailing their pale white wakes. *Akagi* had maneuvered so skillfully that not one torpedo scored, and everyone breathed a deep sigh of relief.[9]

The scene had a very different take from inside the planes. Earnest anticipated that his hydraulics might be hit, so he opened his bomb bay doors before he began his run, making sure that he would be able to drop his fish later. He was right, for in a few moments the fighters came in and his hydraulic lines were hit, causing his tail wheel to drop and block the .30-caliber tunnel gun that his radioman, Harry H. Ferrier, was firing. Ferrier remembered "looking over my shoulder to see why he [the turret gunner, Jay D. Manning] had stopped firing. The sight of his slumped and lifeless body startled me. Quite suddenly I was a scared, mature old man at 18."[10] He was still older a minute later when he was hit in the wrist and then grazed on the head and knocked out, his last sight his blood covering his useless machine gun. The red tabs in the plane's wings popped up, indicating that they were unlocked and free to fold back, but fortunately they didn't. The elevator control was hit and the plane plunged for the water. Earnest managed to use his tabs to get the nose far enough up to drop his torpedo in the direction of a cruiser that crossed his line of sight and then worked his way out of the melee. Of the six TBFs, only Earnest's plane survived the run.

The army's Martin B-26s had little better time of it than the navy torpedo planes despite their heavier armament and higher speed. Their commander, Captain James Collins, USAAF, "had neglected to tell his men when they took off that they were to execute a bombing mission. Since they had thought they were merely on patrol, they were greatly surprised when they came

Fig. 8 Japanese navy "Zero" fighter takes off from the Japanese carrier *Akagi* in the attack on Pearl Harbor, official U.S. Navy photograph 80-G-182252, National Archives, reprinted with thanks

out of the clouds and saw the enemy fleet on the horizon about twenty miles away and were ordered to attack. They were within four or five miles of their target when six Zeroes broke off their combat with the Navy torpedo planes and headed out to intercept the larger Army craft."[11]

The Zeroes were as aggressive as fire ants. "The six fighters came at us fast, straight in, and I watched until I figured they would start shooting," Collins said, "then I went down fast. They missed us and kept on going. Just then other fighters hit us from the rear, and we never shook them off until the attack was over. Anti-aircraft shells were coming closer, but as long as they were missing we held our course. . . . By this time machine gun and pompom tracers were whizzing around us, and we were in position to choose our angle of attack off the carrier's bow. We slipped between several destroyers and cruisers, turned sharply and headed toward the carrier. The carrier made a quick turn, and put on speed in an effort to swing about head-on to us and so present the narrowest possible target."[12]

The Marauders were still about 2 miles from the carrier when Collins's hydraulic system was shot out. Aiming at the side of the carrier, which was ablaze with gunfire, he dropped his torpedo and "pulled up sharply and shot over the carrier's bow at only a couple of hundred feet. Then I pulled the controls straight back and shot straight up another thousand feet."[13] Collins claimed that his "tail gunner, Technical Sergeant Raymond S. White, got two and maybe three Zeroes during this attack."[14] He limped home and landed with difficulty, unable to get the nose wheel down.

Lieutenant James B. Muri followed Collins into the attack. His gun turret was shot out and the tail gunner was killed. A cushion caught fire, and the plane began to blaze, but Muri still made his run. "We were so low and going so fast that as soon as the torpedo got away I had to turn sharply to get over the carrier's deck. I swung over the bow and then raced back the length of the deck, climbing as I went."[15] His nose gunner raked the deck where Japanese sailors were gathered to watch the show. Like Collins, Muri, his left tire shot out, had to make a crash landing. The plane bumped so hard that it shook the instrument panel out of its mounting. The two other B-26s, piloted by Lieutenant Herbert C. Mayes and Second Lieutenant William S. Watts, were not so lucky and crashed into the sea. Army publicity people, who later claimed that the battle had been won by army air force Flying Fortresses, credited two of the Marauders with a hit. The navy gave only one, and Fuchida none. Fuchida was right. The first torpedo attack from the air was over, with no hits for the loss of seven out of ten aircraft.

After considering the sighting reports on the Japanese carriers, Fletcher at 0607 ordered Admiral Spruance to "proceed southwesterly and attack enemy carriers as soon as definitely located. I will follow as soon as planes [scouts launched early in the morning] are recovered."[16] Because of the limited ranges of the fighters and torpedo planes discussed earlier, Spruance delayed launching his strike and sped toward the enemy, hoping to get as close as possible to give his planes a better chance of getting back to the ship after combat.

By now the teletypes were clattering in the American ready rooms, and while the pilots worked on their navigation, information appeared on the screen:

> Enemy naval units sighted within striking distance.
> This is it.

Base course to 240°.

Enemy main body is now attempting to take Midway.

We are intercepting them.

0625 position, 31° latitude, longitude 176° 29′ enemy bears 239°.

We will begin launching planes after closing to 100 miles of enemy.

Wind, southeast, 5 to 7 knots. We will have to turn away from the Japs to launch.

Pilots man your planes.

Squadron commanders to the bridge.

While *Enterprise* and *Hornet* were speeding toward the enemy and the planes were warming up on the flight deck, "Mitscher summoned the CHAG and the four squadron commanders to a hasty meeting with CDR Apollo Soucek, the air officer."[17] Waldron argued heatedly that fighters should stay with the torpedo planes, but Ring wanted them to fly high cover for the entire air group, 20,000 feet up in the air and far away from sea level, where the torpedo action would be. Waldron lost, and the controversy continued when the two men disagreed strongly about the course the group should take to the target. Waldron argued that when *Kido Butai* discovered that American ships were to the northeast, Nagumo would turn in that direction and that they were best therefore to fly a few points to the north to anticipate this change in course. Ring disagreed again, and told everyone they would go out on a different course. He had his way, according to Roy Gee, a pilot in Bombing 8 that morning, because of "the 'good ole boy' attitude that Mitscher had for Ring, and the fact the squadron C.O.s were hesitant to criticize CHAG in the presence of Mitscher. On the lower level we junior people had little respect for CHAG, but we kept it more or less to ourselves."[18]

At about 0700, 155 miles distant from the enemy, Task Force Sixteen began to launch its planes, keeping those in the air overhead for a deferred departure. The *Hornet* began to put its planes in the air at 0702 in the usual order, fighters first, bombers next, then torpedo planes, Waldron being the last off. Getting the group all together took time and used up a lot of gas. The full group was in the air and departed for the attack at about 0755 on an incorrect course of 265 degrees, far to the north of the interception course of 230–240 degrees to the enemy.[19] Waldron broke radio silence to argue with Ring about half an hour into the flight, and at 0816 he swung left to fly his own course and went directly to the Japanese fleet and the deaths of all his squadron except for the lone survivor.[20]

At 0706 *Enterprise* began to launch, putting the longest-range planes in the air first. The bombers, under Lieutenant Commander Clarence Wade McClusky, Jr., CEAG, went off first and after circling for a time when no other planes got off because of problems on the deck, they were ordered at 0745 to proceed independently toward their target on a course of 231 degrees, distance 142 miles. The *Enterprise* was also assuming that Nagumo would maintain his course toward Midway, and so the course given turned out to be a bit too far south. Only after some delay did some good luck and sharp reasoning by Wade McClusky, the hero of the battle, find the enemy fleet. The deck was straightened out, and the *Enterprise* torpedo planes were on their way separately to the target by 0800, with the fighters following soon after. By then, however, any hopes for a coordinated attack were long gone.

The *Yorktown* strike was held back until its scouts had landed, and at 0840 *Yorktown,* feeling confident that there was no second Japanese carrier fleet lying northwest, began launching, holding its scouting squadron in reserve as a backup. *Yorktown* had been in battle before and had learned how to order its launch so that the shortest-range and slowest planes were in the air first and on their way to the target without wasting gas circling while rendezvousing: "The torpedo planes were directed to proceed immediately towards the objective; and the VSBs ordered to circle overhead for 12 minutes and then proceed to overtake the VT before reaching the enemy. In order to conserve fuel for the VF, they were launched at 0905 with orders to rendezvous enroute. Due to the slow speed of the TBD's and the small fuel capacity of the F4F-4's, the above procedure was deemed expedient, and worked out very well. At 0945 all three squadrons were rendezvoused and the group took the following formation: VT-3 at 1500 feet (just below the cloud base), 2 VF for low coverage at 2500 feet, 4 VF at 5000–6000 feet to protect the VT and low VF, and VB-3 at 16,000 feet."[21]

So by about 0930, Midway time, the full American strike was

on its way, but instead of the critical combined strike, the planes were all over the sky. The *Hornet* group was together until Waldron broke off, but on a course that would take it north of the Japanese fleet. Adding to the confusion, the ten *Enterprise* fighters flying at a high altitude mistook the *Hornet* torpedo planes down low for their own[22] and followed Waldron to the target, getting there at about 0918, long minutes before their own Torpedo 6 planes arrived. But the fighters offered support to neither squadron, circling above the Japanese unchallenged on the up sun side for an hour at 20,000 feet before running low on gas and returning at 1010 to their ship.

Things were not going well for the Japanese either. At 0705, just as the American attack from Midway was taking place, the Japanese Midway strike commander, Lieutenant Joichi Tomonaga, had radioed that a second attack on Midway would be needed to prepare the island for the invasion. Nagumo had a big decision to make at this point. He made it at 0715, without damage from repelling the American attack from Midway and still ignorant of the presence of the American fleet, having heard nothing from his scouts. Torpedoes began to be taken off Kates still aboard his carriers and bombs loaded in their place to prepare for a second attack on facilities at Midway. Contact-fused bombs were substituted for armor-piercing on the Val dive-bombers and the Kate high-level bombers. Then, a few minutes later, at 0728, a Japanese scout reported sighting ten American ships to the northeast, though no carriers. Not until 0820 would the scout report a carrier. But by sometime around 0730

Nagumo was at last alerted to his deadly danger and turned his attention away from Midway to thinking of attacking the American fleet. Consultation with staff dragged on, however, until at 0745 it was finally decided to order that torpedoes be left on torpedo planes not yet reloaded to prepare to attack the American fleet. But the attack was to be delayed until the returning Midway strike landed and the air groups from all four carriers could be rearmed and sent out to destroy the American fleet.

This delay was fatal and cost the Japanese a chance to win the battle, though part of the American air attack was already in the air. At 0837 the Japanese commenced bringing the returning Midway strike aboard. After hearing from a scout that ten torpedo planes—presumably a miscounted Torpedo 8—were on the way to attack him, Nagumo at 0855 ordered a turn north to attack the American fleet. It was executed by 0917, when all his Midway strike planes were back aboard. At this point all of his hangar decks were cluttered with planes being refueled and serviced; bombs, torpedoes, and ammunition were scattered about everywhere. It was no moment for the sighting of the fifteen planes of Torpedo 8, some 20 miles distant. All that could be done was to hurry rearming, keeping the attack planes on the hangar decks while using the flight decks to launch additional Zero fighters to deal with the incoming torpedo squadron.

Waldron had bet that the Japanese would turn north when they became aware of the American fleet, and he found them at 0917 immediately after they had made a turn northeast to 70 degrees. Already concerned about his fuel gauge and beset at once by Zeroes, Waldron could not wait for support to show up. He disposed his fifteen planes together in two divisions, each flying in a vee. He started a run on the *Soryu* at 0925. Leroy Quillen, a gunner in Bombing 8, who had heard Waldron on the radio many times and recognized his voice, heard him on the air: "Johnny One to Johnny Two. . . . How'm I doing Dobbs? . . . Attack immediately! . . . I'd give a million to know who done that. . . . There's two fighters in the water. . . . My two wingmen are going in the water."[23]

From the deck of the *Akagi* the destruction was admired in characteristic Japanese fashion for its combination of beauty and bloodiness: "The first enemy carrier planes to attack were 15 torpedo bombers. When first spotted by our screening ships and combat air patrol, they were still not visible from the carriers, but they soon appeared as tiny dark specks in the blue sky, a little above the horizon, on *Akagi*'s starboard bow. The distant wings flashed in the sun. Occasionally one of the specks burst into a spark of flame and trailed black smoke as it fell into the water. Our fighters were on the job, and the enemy again seemed to be without fighter protection. Presently a report came in from a Zero group leader: 'All 15 enemy torpedo bombers shot down.' Nearly 50 Zeros had gone to intercept the unprotected enemy formation! Small wonder that it did not get through."[24]

Waldron went early, trying to escape from a fiery cockpit, and one by one the others dropped into the water. The old TBDs could neither run nor fight it out with their puny armament and plugged ahead until only Gay, his gunner dead and his plane shot up, was left to go in and make the attack that Waldron had decreed to be the duty of his pilots even if only one of them was left. Gay's words, years later, still retain something of the desperation he must have felt after he watched the last two other planes go down:

> My target, which I think was the *Kaga,* was now in a hard turn to starboard and I was going toward its forward port quarter. I figured that by the time a torpedo could travel the distance it should be in the water, the ship should be broadside. I aimed about one quarter of the ship's length ahead of its bow, and reached out with my left hand to pull back the throttle. It had been calculated that we should be at about 80 knots when we dropped these things, so I had to slow down. . . . I was simply trying to do what I had come out to do. When I figured that I had things about as good as I was going to get them, I punched the torpedo release button.
>
> Nothing happened. "Damn those tracers," I thought. "They've goofed up my electrical release and I'm getting inside my range." I had been told that the ideal drop was 1,000 yards range, 80 knots speed, and 80 feet or so of altitude. But by the time I got the control stick between my knees and put my left hand on top of it to fly the plane, and reached across to pull the cable release with my good

right hand, I was into about 850 yards. The cable, or mechanical release, came out of the instrument panel on the
left side, designed to be pulled with the left hand. But those
damn Zeros had messed up my program. My left hand did
not work. Anyhow, it was awkward, and I almost lost control of the plane trying to pull out that cable by the roots.
I can't honestly say I got rid of that torpedo. It felt like it.
I had never done it before so I couldn't be sure and with
the plane pitching like a bronco, I had to be content with
trying my best.

"Okay, so I've gotten rid of the G.D. torpedo. Now what
do I do?"[25]

In a moment Gay was in the water, hiding under the seat cushion that he had saved from the wreckage of his plane, just as
Waldron had told him to save everything because you could
never tell when it would come in handy.

On board the *Enterprise* "an unfortunate chain of circumstances," as Murray called them in his after-action report, began
when his dive-bombers departed alone on a course that would
take them south of the Japanese for a time. The chain continued
when the ten VF-6 fighters, led by Lieutenant Jim Gray, followed
the wrong torpedo squadron, Torpedo 8, to the target, and then
circled at 20,000 feet, apparently unaware of the slaughter taking place below him. At 1010, after his charge, the "real" Torpedo 6, had arrived on the scene and begun its attack, Gray
reported back to the *Enterprise* that he had had an uneventful

flight and being short of gas was returning to base. In that message he finally located the Japanese fleet and described it, something he should have done an hour before when he first saw it. His was by no means the only communication failure that day, and the American admirals after the Catalina sighting reports operated with minimal information about the location of the enemy.

The *Enterprise* torpedo planes, VT-6, commanded by the handicapped Lindsey, flew alone on a course that brought them in 30 miles south of the carriers. They turned north, breaking into two sections for an anvil attack on *Kaga* at 1020. They encountered the first ring of defense ships about 10 miles out and the antiaircraft fire became heavier as the inner defense ring picked them up at 5 miles. By then the Zeroes were among them and began shooting them down. They continued to close in, but as they did so their target turned to starboard, keeping its quarter to the planes. This dance of death was sketched (see fig. 9) by Lieutenant Laub, the senior survivor of the squadron, making clear how the maneuvering of the ships kept the torpedo planes circling, trying vainly, at their slow speed, to get in position to turn in for a broadside run from close enough to be able to launch their torpedoes at an angle of less than 70 degrees. But, Laub says, "the [ship's] turns were so timed that it was impossible to obtain an advantageous point from which to drop."[26]

All this time, of course, the Torpedo 6 planes were being shot down by the Zeroes and battered by the antiaircraft fire. The

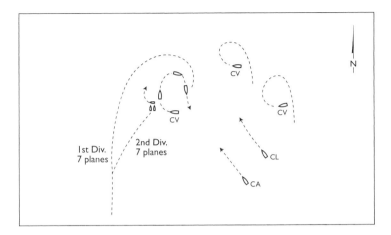

Fig. 9 Sketch drawn by Lieutenant (jg) Robert E. Laub of the attack by Torpedo 6 on the Japanese carriers, redrawn from Laub, "Torpedo Plane Operations in the Air Battle of Midway, June 4, 1942," a description of the major failures of the torpedo planes and their weapon

Enterprise dive-bombers arrived as its surviving torpedo planes were clearing the area. Of the fourteen Torpedo 6 planes, only five survived, one of which, flown by Machinist Albert W. Winchell, crashed in the water on the way back from the attack. First reported as a casualty, he was picked up with his radioman 17 days later, both unharmed but many pounds lighter.

The twelve planes of the *Yorktown* torpedo squadron, VT-3, led by Lieutenant Commander Lance Massey, accompanied by six fighters, arrived at 1015, 20–25 miles out, while Torpedo 6 was still engaged. The Zeroes soon came at them, announcing that they were there for business by dropping their belly tanks

through the few escort Wildcats. The *Yorktown* group had arrived in a bunch, and the dive-bombers of Bombing 3 began
attacking the *Soryu* at once, but Massey, rather than taking advantage of this diversion, chose to lead his torpedo planes, followed by a swarm of Zeroes, toward the *Hiryu*, which was moving off alone toward the north, unseen and unattacked by the
dive-bombers. One can only speculate, but Massey, faced with
a difficult attack problem, must have felt confident that his torpedo planes with their six fighter escorts could on their own
take care of the fourth carrier, lest it escape, as it eventually did.
Later its planes crippled the *Yorktown*. Massey's own fighters
soon left him after losing one plane and being overwhelmed
by the Zeroes. After that the Zeroes chewed at their leisure on
Torpedo 3. Wilhelm G. ("Doc") Esders, an enlisted chief aviation pilot, was one of only two pilots from the twelve Torpedo 3
TBDs to survive this attack, and his after-action report provides
a forceful account of what it was actually like to fly out to the
Japanese carriers, attack, and then make your way back with a
damaged plane and a dying radioman:

> We sighted three dense columns of smoke to our north-
> westward, distance about 20 to 25 miles, at which time we
> changed course in that direction. We also started to climb
> again as we were out of the clouds. The squadron com-
> mander led the squadron to the north side of the enemy
> force. We were at an altitude of 2600 feet. When about

14–18 miles from the enemy carriers, 2 Jap fighters commenced attacking us. The squadron remained in combat formation throughout our approach. After the first attack, the squadron commander started maneuvering considerably, losing and gaining altitude slightly and increasing speed. When approximately 10 miles out, 2 more Jap fighters joined in the fight.

At this time I was very engrossed in watching the squadron leader due to our maneuvering and was unable to observe the ships and their movements very well. We proceeded to lose altitude and increased our speed until we were about 50 feet above the water. Several more Jap fighters joined the engagement. Six to eight Jap fighters continually made attacks during our approach.

We were forced to get low before we desired to start our initial approach, therefore being at a handicap due to the lack of speed.

When approximately one mile from the carrier our leader apparently expected to attack, his plane was hit and it crashed into the sea in flames. At the same time he was hit I had to maneuver very violently to avoid tracer bullets from a Jap plane. We made our final turn of our approach and I saw another plane of our formation crash in flames. In the final stages of our attack, I saw only five planes drop their torpedoes. We completed our attack a few minutes after 1000,[27] including my own.

Throughout our approach over the screen we were under heavy AA fire, which appeared to be very ineffective, most of it bursting approximately 800 to 1000 feet beyond the formation. In the early stages of our approach, my plane was hit by gunfire from a Jap fighter causing the CO_2 fire bottle just forward of my knees to explode. In making our torpedo drops we were under constant gun fire from the carrier, which appeared to be ineffective. We dropped our torpedoes between six and eight hundred yards from the target. At this time my radioman called me over the interphone and said he was hit and would be of no further use to ward off fighter attacks.

Immediately after dropping my torpedo, I turned to my right to clear the ship by several hundred yards. The other four planes crossed directly ahead of the bow of the carrier, one of them crashing into the sea, fighters were still making continuous attacks on us. Due to continuous fighter attacks I was unable to observe the torpedo tracks or if we scored any hits. In making my retreat I was attacked by two fighters immediately after I started my turn to the right. They each made two or three passes at me, then two other fighters came in from ahead, one from the bow and one dead ahead. At that time I was 10 to 12 miles from the carrier we attacked. Two more Jap fighters started making passes at us, one from the port and the other from ahead. They continued to make passes at us until we were about 20 miles from our objective, the fighters then retired toward the Jap fleet.[28]

Lloyd Childers, the wounded gunner for the other Torpedo 3 survivor, Machinist Harry Corl, describes what it was like in the back seat trying to hold off the frenzied Zero attackers:

That was the beginning of the melee with about 30 Zeroes going crazy in the most undisciplined, uncoordinated attack that could be imagined. The estimate of 30 Zeroes was my answer to Corl a few days later when he was writing his report. I got a couple of no deflection shots on crazy Zero pilots who were in a hellava hurry to shoot us down. I fired about 200 rounds or two cans of ammo as we moved in on the target. I observed the F4F's above us mixing it up with the Zeroes. At one point, when I was not shooting at a Zero, I saw a Zero coming almost straight down, not smoking, smacking the water within a hundred yards of us. So, I knew the F4Fs were not losing every encounter, even tho badly outnumbered. I saw other aircraft fall out of the sky, but I could not tell whether ours or theirs. I recall thinking, "My God, this is just like watching a movie." Altho it required some stretching by me, I tried to see what we were headed into. One look showed me three carriers, cruisers and destroyers going top speed and turning. It was an awesome sight that frightened me badly. By this time the AA fire was coming at us in multiple black puffs.

Corl yelled in his high pitched voice, "Look at the skip-per." I looked to the port just in time to see the skipper's plane hit the water in flames, caused by a direct AA hit I assumed.[29]

Childers remembers his pilot saying over the interphone, "We're not going to make it." They did, however, but could not land on the *Yorktown*'s flight deck because of a bomb hole caused by the Japanese dive-bomber attack that was progressing as they returned. His strength sapped by his wound, Childers was able to swim only a few strokes after they crash-landed in the water, but he remembers reaching up and patting the old TBD on the tail as it sank and thanking it for bringing them back.

Fuchida was still on deck on the *Akagi*, watching Torpedo 6 and then Torpedo 3 come in. His memory of details is not perfect, but his description of the remarkable scene is told vividly and with great feeling:

Again at 0930 a lookout atop the bridge yelled: "Enemy torpedo bombers, 30 degrees to starboard, coming in low!" This was followed by another cry from a port look-out forward: "Enemy torpedo planes approaching 40 degrees to port!"

The raiders closed in from both sides, barely skimming over the water. Flying in single columns, they were within five miles and seemed to be aiming straight for *Akagi*. I watched in breathless suspense, thinking how impossible it would be to dodge all their torpedoes. But these raiders, too, without protective escorts, were already being engaged by our fighters. On *Akagi*'s flight deck all attention was fixed on the dramatic scene unfolding before us, and there was wild cheering and whistling as the raiders went down one after another.

Of the 14 [Torpedo 6] enemy torpedo bombers which came in from starboard, half were shot down, and only 5 remained of the original 12 planes [VT-3?] to port. The survivors kept charging in as *Akagi* opened fire with anti-aircraft machine guns. Both enemy groups reached their release points, and we watched for the splash of torpedoes aimed at *Akagi*. But, to our surprise, no drops were made. At the last moment the planes appeared to forsake *Akagi*, zoomed overhead, and made to port and astern of us. As the enemy planes passed *Akagi*, its gunners regained their composure and opened a sweeping fire, in which *Hiryu* joined. Through all this deadly gunfire the Zeros kept after the Americans, continually reducing their number.

Seven enemy planes finally succeeded in launching their torpedoes at *Hiryu*, five from its starboard side and two from port. Our Zeros tenaciously pursued the retiring attackers as far as they could. *Hiryu* turned sharply to starboard to evade the torpedoes, and we watched anxiously to see if any would find their mark. A deep sigh of relief went up when no explosion occurred, and *Hiryu* soon turned its head to port and resumed its original course.

A total of more than 40 enemy torpedo planes had been thrown against us in these attacks, but only seven American planes had survived long enough to release their missiles, and not a single hit had been scored. Nearly all of the raiding enemy planes were brought down.[30]

The torpedo attack from the American carriers was over by 1045, having taken an hour and a half from start to finish and costing almost all the planes and their crews.

Before the water closed over the last Torpedo 6 Devastators, however, the dive-bombers from *Enterprise* arrived like the U.S. Cavalry in a Western. Wade McClusky, CEAG, leading the *Enterprise* dive-bombers, had flown as far west as fuel would allow without sighting the Japanese ships, when, "Call it fate, luck or what you may, . . . at 0955 I spied a lone Jap cruiser [actually the destroyer *Arashi*] scurrying under full power to the northeast. Concluding that it possibly was a liaison ship between the occupation forces and the striking force, I altered my Group's course to that of the cruiser. At 1005 that decision paid dividends. Peering through my binoculars which were practically glued to my eyes, I saw dead ahead about 35 miles distant the welcome sight of the Jap carrier striking force."[31]

The *Yorktown* bombers had arrived about the same time, and between them they polished off *Akagi, Kaga,* and *Soryu.* Commander Tom Cheek, then a Fighting 3 pilot providing defense for the Torpedo 3 planes, watched the great fleet die, taking an empire with it.

As I looked back to *Akagi,* hell literally broke loose.

First the orange-colored flash of a bomb burst appeared on the flight deck midway between the island structure and the stern. Then in rapid succession followed a bomb burst midship, and the water founts of near misses plumed up near the stern. Almost in unison on my left *Kaga's* flight deck erupted with bomb bursts and flames. My gaze remained on *Akagi* as an explosion at the midship waterline seemed to open the bowels of the ship in a rolling, greenish-yellow ball of flame. A black cloud of smoke drew my attention to *Soryu,* still in a turn to starboard, it too was being heavily hit. Dense black smoke billowed from the entire length of its hull. All three ships had lost their foaming white bow waves and appeared to be losing way.

I circled slowly to the right; awe-struck; my mind trying desperately to grasp the full impact of what I had just witnessed, and the scene still in motion. In reading the script, the briefing team had voiced this destructive happening as only a hoped-for possibility. The infernos I now watched in creation were not being viewed from a comfortable seat in a movie, but from atop a parachute pack in a Grumman fighter. . . .

A last look in their direction found the three carriers now almost dead in the water. Each vessel's position was marked by a black cloud of smoke towering above that rolled and boiled in a manner indicating it rose from an area of intense heat.[32]

In the end it was indeed a famous victory, but it cost the torpedo squadrons almost everything. Gay tried to salvage what he could with a belief that the destruction of Torpedo 8 diverted the Zeroes and left a clear sky for the *Yorktown* and *Enterprise* dive-bombers when they did finally arrive: "Figuring the total loss of Torpedo 8 as a staggering blow, it must be remembered in the final figures for the day, our squadron did very well indeed. VT-8 drew down the Zeroes so that the dive bombers had a better chance—and they did a magnificent job."[33] Recent historians have, however, justified the torpedo attacks in a somewhat different way. The deck-spotting procedures of the Japanese carriers meant that the torpedo attacks forced them to use their flight decks during the approximately hour-and-a-half the torpedo squadrons were coming in to launch and land fighters, maintaining the maximum number of armed Zeroes in the air. As a result they could not find the forty-five minutes needed to get their bombers and torpedo planes up from the hangar decks and send them out to attack the American fleet. Even the slow pace of our torpedo attacks and the staggered arrival of the squadrons, though they were tactical failures, maximized the time that Japanese flight decks were tied up. No one can claim credit for this critical effect, totally unintended if unrecognized for sixty years, except the air crews whose blazing courage and sense of duty flew their old planes with their defective torpedoes, without flinching, to a desperate end.[34]

SEVEN

"The Best-Laid Schemes o' Mice an' Men Gang Aft Agley": Command Failures

The poet Robert Burns put it well, and after a famous victory in which his planes were scattered all over the Pacific skies, Admiral Spruance, with equal rue, agreed: "In reading the account of what happened on 4 June, I am more than ever impressed with the part that good or bad fortune sometimes plays in tactical engagements. . . . [Fuchida and Okumiya in *Midway, the Battle That Doomed Japan*] give us credit, where no credit is due, for being able to choose the exact time for our attack on the Japanese carriers when they were at the greatest disadvantage—flight decks full of aircraft fueled, armed and ready to go. All that I can claim credit for, myself, is a very keen sense of the urgent need for surprise and a strong desire to hit the enemy carriers with our full strength as early as we could reach them."[1]

But there were errors and failed judgments as well as luck at work at Midway, and they had a lot to do with the disaster that overtook the torpedo squadrons on June 4. Fate began to weave its web long before the battle when the Devastators were de-signed and the Zero and Wildcat came off the drawing boards; when torpedoes were not built in sufficient numbers or tested effectively at Goat Island; when pilots were not trained to drop them because of their cost; and on and on, a fatal web that was completely in place by 0700 in the Pacific waters northwest of Midway Island, on June 4, 1942.

It can be argued, of course, that the old Devastators and their faulty torpedoes should never have been sent out on such a dan-gerous mission as attacking *Kido Butai*. Yet the answer to that would surely have to be that they were what we had, and that torpedo planes, whatever problems might be known but not fully factored into tactical thinking, were officially considered to be ship killers, delivering the heavy knockout blows in a car-rier concerted attack.

But with all the technological weaknesses, it need not have been as bad a day as it was for the torpedo squadrons if some fatal tactical mistakes had not been made. First came the failure for an almost laughable, if not so tragic, number of reasons of our fighters to protect the torpedo planes. The captain of the *En-terprise* in his official Midway report states that "the loss of such a large number of torpedo planes (10) [out of fourteen from his ship] is attributed to the lack of coordination and support by fighter escort."[2] When enough time had passed for the blood to disappear in the ocean, Admiral Nimitz rehearsed this lesson, with feeling: "TBD planes are fatally inadequate for their pur-pose. The loss of the brave men who unhesitatingly went to their death in them is grievous. The TBF is much improved, but still cannot attack ships defended by fighters without fighter support."[3] He was dead right about the new TBFs. Six of them attacked from Midway without fighter support because the Midway fighters had been reserved to protect the island base. Five of the six were lost and the last was shot to pieces, its gunner killed and its radioman wounded.

It may well be that the commanders on the scene like Murray had tried to provide some support for their torpedo planes, but they had to save as much as possible their fighters for combat air patrol to protect their ships as to support the torpedo planes while they carried out their dangerous task. Probably this was the right choice considering what was at stake, but three groups of torpedo planes went in with no fighter support whatsoever and were butchered by the Zeroes. The last, Torpedo Squadron Three from the *Yorktown,* was accompanied in its attack by six fighters that lost one of their number before fighting their way out while the torpedo planes were being shot down.

On Murray's ship, the *Enterprise,* fighter support was promised but not delivered. Before his squadron left the ship, Lieutenant Commander Lindsey got out of his bunk, where he was recuperating from his earlier crash, and told his Torpedo 6 pilots in the ready room that they could expect fighter support in their attack. Lieutenant Arthur Ely, XO, had arranged, he said, with the fighter leader, Lieutenant J. S. Gray, Jr., of the ten Wildcats from Fighting 6 accompanying the strike, to remain high but then come down fast when Ely or Lindsey called, "Come on down, Jim." But it didn't work. Once in the air, Gray mistook Torpedo 8 for Torpedo 6 and followed Waldron straight to the target. He of course heard no "Come on down, Jim," call from Waldron, and if he saw Waldron's attack, he gave Torpedo 8 no help before he left for home, short on gas.

When Torpedo 6 attacked, Gray was leaving, and Lieutenant Laub, the senior VT-6 survivor, in a later set of recommendations—supplementary to his after-action report—on future torpedo attacks, begins by saying that the absence of fighter support was one of the main causes of the torpedo plane disaster. But then he added sadly that their presence would not have made any difference anyway. The Japanese fighters outclassed the Wildcats: "The fourth factor [in the destruction of VT-6] is believed to be the lack of coordination with fighter escort, who were at an altitude in excess of 20,000 feet at time of attack. Rendezvous with fighters was not effected before departure from ship and none of our fighter protection was seen at any time during the period away from the ship. Too much stress cannot be placed on the lack of coordination of fighter escort [note that these words can be read two ways] since our present fighter is no match for the Japanese Zero-type fighter, and were not present in sufficient numbers to do more than protect themselves."[4] Laub may have been resigned about the fighter support failure, but others were not. When he landed back aboard *Enterprise*, Chief Machinist Steven Smith, "who believed that Lt. Gray was responsible for the frightful losses suffered by Lindsey's men that morning, had to be physically restrained from attacking the fighter squadron skipper."[5] Smith jumped out of his cockpit and headed up the island waving his .45 Colt automatic in his hand. He was shouting that he was going to kill Gray, but nothing more was heard of the matter by those of us who, astonished, watched the scene.

The *Hornet*'s fighters were, if possible, even less effective than those from the *Enterprise*. In a hurried conference on the bridge just before takeoff, Waldron had argued for fighter help, desperately wanted it, but didn't get it. "The skipper had tried in vain to get us fighter protection. He even tried to get one fighter to go with us, or even get one fighter plane and one of us would fly it even though we had never been up in one, but he could not swing it. The fighter boys had never met the Zeros, and from what they had heard from the Coral Sea action it wasn't wise to meet one without altitude. The Group Commander [Stanhope Ring] and the Captain [Mitscher] felt that the SBD's needed more assistance than we did. They had caught hell in the Coral Sea and the torpedo planes had been lucky."[6] In offering to use his own pilots, Waldron was almost surely insinuating that the fighter pilots were afraid to mix it up with the Zeroes, and at least a touch of this fear is around the edges of the overall fighter performance that morning. The fighter ready rooms in the fleet crackled with discussions about how the Wildcat could survive in a fight with a Zero only by using superior altitude to dive through the enemy and keep on going. At any rate, on the bridge of the *Hornet* it was ordered that the ten Fighting 8 F4Fs assigned to the strike were to fly a 20,000-foot-high cover above the dive-bombers, at 10,000 or 12,000 feet, far above the Devastators down at sea level.

After Waldron broke off and flew directly to the Japanese ships, the *Hornet* fighters and bombers remained together and flew a course north of Nagumo, until the fighters, gas running low, turned back as the result of another piece of insubordination, not unlike Waldron's, though for a different purpose. Ensign John McInerney, after twice flying up to the fighter commander, Lieutenant Commander Samuel G. Mitchell, and indicating that they were low on gas, past the point of no return, and being vehemently waved back into formation, broke away on his own with a wingman and turned back toward the ship. The rest of the fighters, including an angry Mitchell, followed him shortly. All of them flew too far south on their return course, missed their carrier — may even have sighted it but failed to recognize it — and had to land in the open ocean without ever seeing the enemy, except maybe some smoke as they passed to the south of the Japanese fleet. So poor was their training that one pilot made a water landing with his wheels down and another landed downwind.[7]

Over on the *Yorktown,* the only American carrier with previous carrier battle experience, Lieutenant Commander John S. Thach, the skipper of the ship's fighting squadron, consulted with Lieutenant Commander Lance E. Massey, the leader of Torpedo 3. They planned on eight fighters accompanying the torpedo planes but had to settle for six. Those in charge had decided not to risk any precious fighters that day, though they were later persuaded to send out the six. One of the pilots in the fighter ready room on the *Yorktown* before takeoff describes what happened. He and the other pilots were working out their navigation, discovering that, "from the standpoint of fuel, the anticipated position of the Japanese force was beyond the effective combat range of our Grumman F4F-4s. Someone else had reached the same conclusion, for shortly an order came down to scratch the VF escort. Torpedo Three would have to go it alone. Thach bolted from the ready room heading up the ladder in the direction of the bridge. Returning half an hour later he erased the names of McCuskey and Bright from the schedule. The escort would go, he announced, less my second section. Six F4Fs would ride herd on VT-3's twelve TBDs."[8] In the event, the fighters were so closely engaged by the Japanese Zeroes that they lost one of their own and had to battle for their lives rather than protect the torpedo planes. Then the torpedo planes were massacred, ten out of twelve. As one historian puts it, "As far as their prime mission, that of protecting VT-3, was concerned, the fighters might as well stayed out of it."[9]

In the end, the torpedo planes for one reason or another went to their destruction unprotected by the fighters, and this was but one part of a more general breakdown of the U.S. Navy carrier tactics on June 4. A standard coordinated strike was assumed, though there is no record of the admirals having discussed it. The full air groups of the *Hornet* and the *Enterprise,* minus the planes needed to protect the carriers, were intended to fly separately to the Japanese carriers but arrive about the same time. In the usual procedure, the fighters would engage the Japanese CAP, which were expected to be at high altitude, the dive-bombers would attack the four carriers, and the torpedo planes would sneak unnoticed into the melee to deliver the coup. About an hour later, if it was clear that there were no concealed Japanese carriers, the *Yorktown* air group, minus its scouting squadron held in reserve, would arrive and mop up what was left of the Japanese fleet.

Instead, the torpedo planes went in first, squadron by squadron, without any diversion from the fighters or dive-bombers. The *Yorktown* dive-bombers did attack at nearly the same time as their torpedo planes arrived, but Torpedo 3 went off after the *Hiryu,* some distance to the north, which was not being dive-bombed. Our fighters were all over the skies, but except for Thach's small group, they never engaged the enemy.[10] The *Hornet* dive-bombers never even saw the enemy. The *Enterprise* and *Yorktown* dive-bombers arrived from different directions almost simultaneously, though only by good luck. They had left their respective ships an hour apart, and the *Enterprise* bombers found their way to the target only by following the lone Japanese destroyer below, left behind, by chance heading for the carriers. A coordinated strike was, of course, difficult to execute with planes with very different speeds and ranges taking off from multiple carriers under different commands. No wonder the pilots called them "group gropes," and this was surely the biggest grope of all. But the Japanese executed a similar exercise perfectly from six carriers at Pearl Harbor and from four in the June 4 dawn attack on Midway Island.

The American commanders surely assumed that they were making a concerted attack, but at Midway each admiral, each ship, each air group, and nearly each squadron went its own way. Good old American independence was evident throughout the operation, beginning in the planning stage before the battle. Though the schedule was very tight, planning should have been a priority during the brief time the American carriers were together at Pearl Harbor late in May. After the war Admiral Fletcher, in tactical command of the entire fleet at Midway, complained of the "lack of time for conference, drill, preparation of plans and organizations, etc."[11] Nothing would have been more fruitful than for him to have met with Spruance and for their staffs to have discussed plans and procedures. But they did not. Admiral Nimitz briefed each of the fleet commanders separately, and Fletcher was ordered by Nimitz not to prescribe flight operations for any carrier other than the *Yorktown,* though he was the senior officer present and the only one who had already commanded in a big carrier-versus-carrier battle, the Coral Sea. It is important to note that alone among the carriers that day the *Yorktown*'s operational staff and its air officer, Commander M. E. Arnold, doped out what Nagumo was likely to do and sent their strike out on a course that intercepted the enemy directly, arriving at the same time that squadrons that had gone out an hour earlier also got there. Once the ships were at sea they maintained radio silence, except for transmission of priority information on the short-range talk between ships (TBS) radio frequency, whose privacy was not entirely certain, and the limited information they could exchange by flag and signal light. Though Fletcher was in nominal command of all three carriers at Midway, Spruance operated pretty much on his own. After bombs hit the *Yorktown,* Fletcher transferred to a cruiser and told Spruance that he would follow his movements for the remainder of the battle. Fletcher's after-action report on the battle is short. He was a laconic man who disliked interviews and distrusted journalists. It is not surprising that Spruance rather than Fletcher is usually treated as the victor of Midway, though Fletcher was the senior officer present and formally in command.

This "go-it-alone" attitude extended throughout the fleet, but nowhere more obviously or catastrophically than on the *Hornet.* Because it had no admiral aboard when it sailed, the *Hornet* lacked some of the most secret codes that would have permitted it to read radio messages from Nimitz in Pearl and King back in Washington, D.C.[12] On the *Enterprise,* Captain Miles Browning, Spruance's staff air officer, to say the least an eccentric and erratic officer, was slow and very remiss throughout the three days of the battle in telling the other carrier for which Spruance was responsible, the *Hornet,* what it was supposed to do.[13] On the morning of June 4, although Browning knew by 0600 that the combined strike was to be launched at 0700, he neglected to inform *Hornet* until just before that hour.

Some of the confusion on the *Hornet* throughout the day can be traced back to late orders and lack of timely information.

Face-to-face dissent exploded on the *Hornet* bridge at the meeting, mentioned earlier, of the captain, the group commander, the squadron commanders, and others just before the attack was launched. After the discussion about fighter protection, there was a blowup about the course to be flown to the enemy. Waldron had already talked to his pilots about what he considered to be the most direct course to the enemy carriers: "Before we left the ship, Lt. Comdr. Waldron told us that he thought the Japanese Task Forces would swing together when they found out that our Navy was there and that they would either make a retirement just far enough so that they could again retrieve their planes that went in on the attack and he did not think that they'd go on into the Island of Midway as most of the squadron commanders figured."[14] A direct course to the enemy was about 230 or 235 degrees, but Waldron's thinking would have indicated something at least up around 240. He must have explained his reasons for his preferred attack course, but Ring asked all the squadron commanders to work out their own headings. This highly irregular democratic procedure led to several different courses. Ring settled the matter by choosing still another course, 265 degrees, much too far north to find any enemy ships.[15] To this day no one has offered a satisfactory explanation of this colossal error that removed the *Hornet*'s large strike group, one-third of the available force, from the attack on the Japanese carriers. Ring did not write an after-action report, itself an unheard of and unexplained omission, or at least it has never been made available.[16]

The *Hornet* started launching at 0700 and sent off the planes in the usual order, fighters first, then bombers, finally torpedo planes. Executing the standard "deferred departure" that was ordered by the *Enterprise,* the group circled, burning gas the fighters could not spare, until all planes were airborne, and then went off together at about 0755 on a course of 265 degrees. About half an hour out, Waldron, flying low with Torpedo 8, after his nasty radio exchange with Ring about the proper course, broke away from the fighters and bombers and took his squadron off on a southwesterly course that led him straight to the enemy fleet and his squadron's destruction.

Ring with his two squadrons of dive-bombers and his ten Wildcats flew on west, until the fighters, past their point of no return, broke off on their own to try to return to base. Bombing 8 then decided that Nagumo lay to the south and turned in that direction on their own, eventually splitting into two groups, one of which landed on Midway, the other returning to the ship. The scouting squadron, 228 miles out and running short on gas, eventually turned back, on its own, and returned to the ship, bombs still aboard. Ring followed after a delay. During all this time no plane in the *Hornet* strike group other than the torpedo planes saw anything more than smoke near Nagumo's fleet, and this no one chose to investigate. Ring's SBD had barely stopped rolling on the *Hornet* deck when someone notified him that Mitscher wanted to see him. Still in his flight gear he raced up to the bridge, where, according to the scuttlebutt, his superiors chewed him out royally for having "screwed up" big time. (See fig. 10 for the courses flown by the *Hornet* planes on the morning of June 4.)

On the *Enterprise* the attack group was also split up. At 0706 the strike group began to take off, bombers first. *Enterprise* squadrons were also supposed to make a "deferred departure," but as the bombers circled, a delay on deck prevented the fighters and torpedo planes from launching, and at 0745 the bombers were ordered to depart alone. The fighters got off soon after, and then the torpedo planes by 0800, nearly an hour after the launch began. Once in the air, the fighters, moving much faster and higher than their own torpedo planes, mistook and followed Waldron and Torpedo 8, already broken off from their own air group. The three *Enterprise* groups, bombers, fighters, and torpedo planes, were by then all proceeding entirely independently.

Task Force Seventeen operated separately from Task Force Sixteen, about 10 miles away, so that it would be difficult to attack all the carriers at the same time. Fletcher launched his strike from the *Yorktown* between 0840 and 0905. The bombers circled while the torpedo planes took off, and then they departed together for the target on a course of 240 degrees. The six escorts of VF-3 went last and caught up on the way to the target. The enemy was sighted about 1020, and the torpedo attack began about 1030, accompanied by six fighters. The bombers went in about 1025 but Massey's torpedo planes settled on another carrier to attack. The torpedo planes did not survive, but the *Yorktown*'s squadrons did manage something like a coordinated attack, by far the most efficient American air operation of the morning.

On the whole what was intended to be a precisely coordinated attack ended as a scramble. No wonder historians have spoken of the "miracle" or the "tarnished" or "incredible victory" of Midway, though their meaning was different from mine. Where they thought of the victory as a triumph of a smaller force against a larger and better prepared, my sense of the words is that we triumphed incredibly over big defects in technology and gross errors in tactical operations. There were other losses, but in the end the torpedo planes paid the highest price for this breakdown of coordinated strike procedures. The numbers bear repeating. In all fifty-one torpedo planes tried to hit the Japanese ships. Only seven torpedo planes landed back at base. The *Enterprise* got four of its planes back, and three Midway planes returned to the island, one navy, two army, all badly shot up. Two of the *Yorktown* planes made it back but landed in the water. The two crews were picked up, though the gunner of one later died from wounds.

There were other problems at Midway. Communications and scouting were, frankly, a mess. The overall plan was set by Cincpac, which, to maintain secrecy, did not tell Midway that our carriers were lying in wait for the Japanese. The Midway scouts, PBY squadrons, were to report their sightings to Midway, which would then forward them in the clear by a still-operating cable to Cincpac, which would in turn send them to the American carriers. No one considered that the delay involved could be fatal in carrier warfare, which depended on split-second timing. Fortunately, our fleet picked up the sighting report of 0552 directly, but the relay came through only at 0623 Midway time, thirty-one minutes later.

The PBY Catalinas, however, had no instructions to send further reports of the Japanese fleet's movements, and the American carriers labored without additional scouting reports until their own planes attacked. During this time the Japanese, unreported, made their critical turn north, which threw off some of the attacking force, and no more than two Japanese carriers were ever reported all day. The fourth and last, the *Hiryu*, was discovered only when its planes attacked the *Yorktown*. This disaster is detailed by John Lundstrom (7 September 2005, BOMRT, www.midway42.org).

By contrast, the Japanese scouts, once they found the American carriers, stayed with them even after they were running out of gas, and they reported to Nagume, too late of course, the movements of the American fleet and its composition. One scout even sighted Waldron's Torpedo Squadron Eight incoming on its attack and sounded the alarm, which got the Zero CAP down at sea level, where they slaughtered the Americans. The Japanese, despite their neglect of the carrier-based scouts, were much ahead in training the catapult-fired scouts on their cruisers in their duties, and the long range of their planes made their searches very effective.

The *Yorktown* doped out what was happening better than the other ships and sent its planes directly to the target. But Fletcher did not share his knowledge about the best launching order with Spruance, and Spruance didn't tell the *Hornet* what he knew, and Marc Mitscher said that he did not tell his planes in the air that he had heard that the Japanese had changed course: "About one hour after the planes had departed, the enemy reversed his course and started his retirement. We did not break radio silence to report this to the planes."[17]

EIGHT

"Sorry about That": Survival

By June 5 the Japanese were on their way back to Japan, Midway Island was still in American hands, and one of the world's great naval battles was over. The ocean was dotted with bright yellow Mae Wests and life rafts of the survivors. These would know their fate early along; others would wait a lifetime.

Ensign Wesley F. Osmus of Torpedo Squadron Three was one of the first survivors to be picked up, but by the wrong people. Osmus had survived the attack, though his radioman did not, and had flown southwest some distance before he crashed at about 1100. His plane was badly shot up, and he was trying to make Midway Island, probably reasoning that he was too damaged to land back aboard a carrier. He swam for some time in his Mae West until he was spotted by a lookout on the Japanese destroyer *Arashi*. It had been left behind to pursue a hunt for the American submarine *Nautilus*, which had made a run on the Japanese carriers in the morning. The search was fruitless, and as *Arashi* turned north to catch up with the fleet, Osmus was sighted and brought aboard to be interrogated about the American carrier force, of which the Japanese still knew little. It was at about this time that *Arashi* was spotted by McClusky, 20,000 feet above, and used as a guide to the Japanese fleet.

Osmus was twenty-three, from Chicago. "The Japanese . . . saw a stocky, somewhat bewildered, dark-haired flier. He had minor burns on his hands, face, and arms, apparently incurred during the final moments of his Devastator flight, and he was tired from swimming."[1] The captain of the destroyer and the commander of its flotilla remained out of sight and called questions to an interrogator, the torpedo officer, who unnerved Osmus by waving his sword while interrogating him. He spoke only a little English but wrote down his superiors' questions about the makeup of the American fleet.[2] The *Arashi,* having rejoined *Kido Butai,* went alongside the mortally wounded *Akagi* to help with damage control. Toward sunset, by which time it was clear that three and probably all four of the Japanese carriers were going to sink, Japanese tempers must have been as short as their hopes of destroying the American navy. Osmus was taken to the fantail and dispatched with a fire ax to the back of the head. He did not die at once but clung to the rail until his fingers were smashed and he dropped into the ocean and drowned. His treatment was brutal by our standards but accorded with Shinto racism and the samurai warrior code of Bushido, in which "defeat was viewed as shameful; surrender was dishonorable; compassion for defeated enemies, male or female, was weakness; and those who surrendered were worthy only of contempt."[3] Our war crimes investigators held a very different moral view of surrender but were not able after the war to establish who gave the order to kill Osmus. The surviving crewmembers—*Arashi* was sunk on August 6, 1943, at the Battle of Vella Gulf—admitted no responsibility. They did remember keeping Osmus's personal possessions, a wallet, a pen, and a picture of a girl, but did not know what happened to them.[4]

The battle having moved on out of his sight, but not his imagination, George Gay, the only survivor of the Torpedo 8 attack from the *Hornet,* got in his life raft and was picked up the next day by a Catalina from Midway and transferred to a hospital in Pearl Harbor. Billed as the "sole survivor of Torpedo 8," he became a national hero.[5] Admiral Nimitz sent a high-ranking officer to interview him, and he provided a stirring description of the battle, remembering unlikely things like seeing a PBY kill three Japanese near him with machine-gun fire, hitting a carrier with his torpedo, and a sensational view of the destruction of the Japanese carriers, which he was most unlikely to have seen from his head-level position in the waves since the ships would have moved rapidly away from him as the battle progressed.

He had other visitors as well, Nimitz himself, and another torpedo pilot who had found a less heroic way of surviving. Before Torpedo 8 left Pearl Harbor to fly out to the *Hornet* for the coming battle, there was a strange incident that Gay later reported in the following way. "Frenchie Fayle went out into a sugar cane field alone. He came back with a deep knife wound in his right leg just below the knee, saying he had fallen off a big lava rock. That put him in the hospital and out of action."[6] Gay says only that Fayle was "visibly shaken" when told about the attack. Fayle did live to fight another day in the Solomons, but Torpedo Squadron 8 never forgave him, and sixty years later on their Web site, old Torpedo 8 hands still made sure the world knows what he did.[7]

George Gay was, if not the sole survivor of Torpedo 8, the most famous survivor of Midway. After he was rescued he toured the country for the war effort, as the propaganda machine liked to be called, and got his picture, with a wicked smirk, on the cover of *Life* magazine. After the war he became a pilot for TWA. He did not write his memoirs until 1979, when he holed up in a motel room in Naples, Florida, fending off a lawyer who had bought the motel and wanted to evict him, long enough to tell his story.[8] He felt that he could finish *Sole Survivor* only in the place where he had begun it. He had saved documents over the years: his Pearl Harbor "Interview," Mears's book *Carrier Combat,* and a copy of the report he made in the hospital, and he copied sections freely and without attribution from these sources. His memory had also flourished luxuriantly over the years, so much so that historians consider his book to some degree at least untrustworthy, though it is the only personal record we have of Torpedo 8 on the way to its destruction. He chose to publish privately and himself distribute *Sole Survivor: The Battle of Midway and Its Effect on His Life.* Presumably his story would have attracted any publisher in the country, but the book is poorly written and abominably edited, so it may be that he was defensive about his writing. In the 1960s and 1970s he believed, like many others, that the country had gone to the dogs, and copies of this book carry an inscription: "May each of you who reads this be as lucky as I was at Midway. George Gay, Keep America Strong." So he may have published to support rearmament. When Gay died, his ashes were put in the ocean on August 31, 1995, near where Torpedo 8 was wiped out fifty-three years earlier.

A lifeboat turned up filled with Japanese black gang sailors who had emerged from the engine room of a sinking carrier to find their ship abandoned. It took days for the eight surviving pilots out of ten from Fighting 8 to be located and picked up, since the searchers had wrong information about the likely point where they ditched. Of this more in a moment. A former enlisted pilot in Torpedo 6, Machinist Albert W. Winchell, and his gunner, Douglas M. Cossitt, crashed on their way back from the June 4 attack. Down to skin and bones they survived for seventeen days in a life raft without emergency rations, which were lost in landing. When I later saw him at Pearl Harbor, Winchell gave me back a cigarette lighter with a long wick he had borrowed when he walked out to his plane to take off. The wick glowed rather than flaming and could therefore be used in the wind. He said it had been very useful, but when I thought about it I couldn't imagine what use it could have been with no emergency rations and no cigarettes.

But not all the Midway survivors had been in the water, and rescue was for some of them a complicated matter. The brass on the *Hornet* particularly had a big problem. John Lundstrom, a distinguished historian of the Pacific War, once said that could he have been at Midway on June 4, 1942, the first day of the battle, he would want to have been on the bridge of the USS *Hornet.*[9] Not because everything went right on the *Hornet* that day, rather the opposite: everything went wrong. The ship's fighters gave its torpedo planes no protection, got lost, ran out of gas, and ditched without firing a shot; its dive-bombers never sighted the enemy fleet, returning with bombs still on their racks; and its torpedo squadron was wiped out without getting a hit. Official records, after-action reports, awards of decorations, personal memoirs, and communication logs have, with silence, ambiguous language, and open contradictions, obscured the *Hornet*'s failures so completely that over time they have almost been lost in the fog of the past. Which may well have been what the writers of the records sought in the first place.

Marc Mitscher, commanding officer of the *Hornet,* thought for a time that his career was over, so badly had his air group performed. Commander Stanhope Ring, the leader of the air group, might well have seen himself commanding a dry dock somewhere out in the boondocks, which is what happened to Commander Joseph J. Rochefort, the brilliant Hypo cryptanalyst — the MVP of the battle — when he fell afoul of Washington. How after all to explain such a big-time mistake that had thrown away one-third of the American strike force in what came to be known as "the flight to nowhere"? Lifetime navy careers were at stake, and a cover-up began soon after the battle.

Mandatory after-action reports were explicitly required on a standard navy form dedicated to this purpose: "(a) To be filled out by unit commander immediately upon landing after each action or operation in contact with the enemy. (b) Do not 'gun deck' this report — if data can not be estimated with reasonable accuracy enter a dash in space for which no data is available."[10]

But there are no appropriate reports for Ring's *Hornet* air group. The only immediate description of what happened to Torpedo 8 is Ensign Gay's interview conducted at the command of Cincpac in the hospital in Pearl Harbor on June 7. A fighting squadron report attached to the ship's report was written by Lieutenant Commander Jimmy Thach, who had been transferred to the *Hornet* on June 5 from the *Yorktown* to command the remainder of Fighting 8. He reported, very summarily, not on Fighting 8, about which he could have known little, but on the actions of VF-3 and the six fighters he led in close support of VT-3, the *Yorktown*'s torpedo squadron. It is difficult to understand why this report was enclosed with the *Hornet* after-action report when no other squadron or air group reports were attached. Perhaps it was thought that it would lend substance to a report with lots of gaps.

Marc Mitscher's after-action report for the entire ship, the *Hornet,* was the only official report of what had happened on CV-8 during the Battle of Midway. Mitscher says correctly that the position of the enemy at the time of launch was "155 miles distant, bearing 239° T from this task force." It does not specify the course that Ring and the air group flew but allows readers to

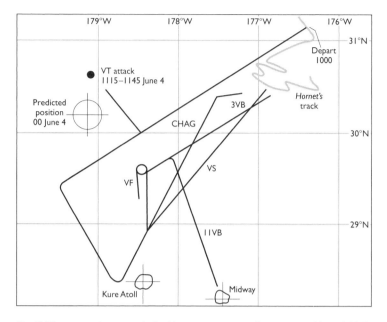

Fig. 10 Map purporting to track the *Hornet* air group on the morning of June 4, 1942, redrawn from attachment to the USS *Hornet*'s after-action report, "Battle of Midway: 4–7 June 1942, Serial 0018 of 13 June 1942"

think that what it calls a "prescribed bearing" was close to the direction given for the enemy. This implication was made specific by a spurious map attached to the report that shows Ring flying south of the Japanese, then turning toward Midway, and then returning to the ship (see fig. 10). This, the report goes on to say, took the *Hornet* planes south of *Kido Butai,* for Nagumo had in the meantime "reversed his course and started his retirement."[11] The implication is that Ring missed the target only because he did not know about this course change. Mitscher's report goes on to say that a radio message was received on the *Hornet* about the Japanese change in course, but *Hornet* "did not break radio silence to report this to the planes."[12] Ring then made the mistake of searching still farther to the south after he crossed the point where he could have expected to encounter Nagumo. Had Ring "turned north, contact would probably have been made," Mitscher concludes.

The effect of the report, by omission and indirection, was to transform Ring's huge error into an understandable mistake for which no apologies need be made. The strike flew south of the Japanese because they had turned north; the ship in order to maintain radio silence did not send out information it had received about the Japanese turn north; the strike decided to search for them to the south; the torpedo planes, for unexplained reasons, flew a different course to the enemy. This is all possible, but it ceases to be credible when the map shows the fighters turning due north, which makes no sense when they were already low on gas, and then turning south again for some unexplained reason, and then disappearing from the map, somewhere north of Midway. The bombers are shown accompanying them for a time but then breaking off and starting for the ship, only to turn south toward Midway again.

Mitscher's commander, Rear Admiral Raymond Spruance, did not approve of the way the *Hornet* had written its action report, and at the beginning of his own report to Cincpac he casts doubt on Mitscher's accuracy with unusual frankness for such an official, high-level report, and for the old boys' network:

"Where discrepancies exist between *Enterprise* and *Hornet* reports, the *Enterprise* report should be taken as the more accurate."

The map had enough inexplicable oddities to have raised big questions about it and the Mitscher report, but they stood for many years as the official representations of the flight of the *Hornet* air group on the morning of June 4. Many people knew something was wrong,[13] but the matter was never dealt with openly until in the strangest of the Midway rescues a former marine navigator began looking into the death of one of the fighter pilots, Mark Kelly, in the downed *Hornet* group and published his findings along with a splendid and accurate map. Bowen Weisheit, an attorney in Baltimore, was a trustee of the C. Markland Kelly, Jr. Memorial Foundation, set up by the father in honor of his son, who was not among those rescued from the water after the Fighting 8 group was belatedly found. As Weisheit tells the story, several drinks after a meeting of the foundation board late in the last century led to a decision that he was the man to work out just what had in fact happened to Ensign Kelly, whose fate had remained surrounded with mystery. He undertook his task responsibly and expertly, noting at the start that the Fighting 8 pilots who were rescued were found some 300 miles from where the map attached to Mitscher's report indicated they would be. Curious, Weisheit went on to look at all the records, interviewed surviving deck officers and pilots, and came up with the firm conclusion that the map attached

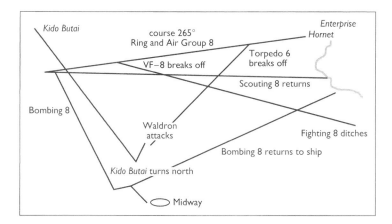

Fig. 11 "Replot of courses flown by elements of USS *Hornet's* air group on the morning of June 4, 1942," adapted and reprinted with the kind permission of Bowen Weisheit from *The Last Flight of Ensign C. Markland Kelly, Junior, USNR, Battle of Midway, June 4, 1942* (1996)

to the Mitscher report was wrong. What actually happened on "the flight to nowhere" is discussed in detail in appendix 3, but in brief, Weisheit concluded that Ring and his planes actually took for reasons he does not try to explain a course of about 265 or 270 degrees, far north of the Japanese (see fig. 11). His torpedo planes, as we have seen, broke off to the left from the main group about half an hour out and flew their own course directly to the target. Ring continued on his original course until, without sighting the enemy, his fighters low on fuel turned back to the southeast, got lost, missed the ship, and ran out of gas. This was where young Kelly was lost. Ring's bombing squadron abandoned him and turned on its own toward Midway. Ring

133

himself returned directly on an almost reciprocal course to the *Hornet* after his scouting squadron turned back.

But no one raised any public questions about all this at the time, and in September 1942, an award ceremony was held on the flight deck of the *Enterprise* at Pearl Harbor. Commander Stanhope Cotton Ring received a Navy Cross for "extraordinary heroism and outstanding devotion to duty" on June 6, not, notice, June 4, the big day of the battle, at Midway, the same decoration that Waldron received posthumously. Ring's radioman was recommended for a Distinguished Flying Cross but reportedly refused it.

Did Mitscher personally invent the story his report and the false map tell to save his reputation and that of his air group commander? Unlikely. His Midway report was surely put together by his subordinates, and there had to have been a lot of collusion or, more likely, quiet agreements among a network of Naval Academy graduates who saw careers as the paramount consideration, not an unfamiliar military point of view. But Mitscher, not a thoughtful man, known for his loyalty to his officers and to the system, signed the report, and he was therefore responsible for all that was in it.[14] He and Ring had worked together at the Bureau of Aeronautics in the 1930s, and he continued to support Ring after the Midway mess, recommending him for captain and for his Navy Cross, and choosing him as his chief of staff in patrol wings he commanded immediately after Midway. Whether he ordered the cover-up or not, he had to have known what was going on. "In 1947, a Naval War College strategic and tactical analysis of the Battle of Midway called attention to the *Hornet* air group's failure to turn *north* [so they accepted the report's statement about the course the air group took!] blaming Mitscher only to the extent that "the commanding officer should insure that flight leaders are properly briefed."[15] But by then Mitscher had been canonized as "The Magnificent Mitscher" for his performance as the commander of big, fast carrier forces later in the war.

Captain Ring, however, never quite lived down his performance on June 4. He was later reported to have said in an officers' club at Pearl Harbor, "The pilots on the *Hornet* think I'm a real shit." Nor did he forget it or the report that covered him. Having failed to file his own required after-action report at Midway, he in effect wrote it, by hand, after the war to exculpate himself from failures he had never been publicly charged with. In March 1946 he stowed his awkward letter in a chest in his closet, where it remained for years until found by his family after his death. The family allowed it to be published only in part by a sympathetic naval officer.[16]

Ring speaks in his letter of flying a "predetermined interception course," but never specifies it, though he blames poor information for causing him to go too far south to find Nagumo's fleet. Nagumo's change of course northward was, he contends, information that the other fellows on the *Enterprise* had and that enabled them to find and sink the enemy:

It is appropriate at this time to interject my understanding that *Enterprise Group* was favored with later information of the whereabouts of the enemy than was *Hornet Group*. Although communications in 1942 were most unreliable between air and surface craft, even though *Hornet* might have broken radio silence to keep the *Group* informed of the latest developments, there was no assurance that such information would have been received by the *Group*. As a matter of fact, I do not believe that *Hornet* received the reported new position of the enemy.[17] Therefore my change of squadrons' course to the south was based entirely on my estimate of the situation (which proved faulty) and not on definite information of the enemy movements.[18]

He confusedly blames the ship for not updating him, and then says that he doubts they knew about the enemy's change of course. Later he says that he tried to round his squadrons up when they became confused about the *Hornet*'s homing signal. In fact they had all left him for one reason and another and proceeded on their own ways. Ring speaks of Waldron only to say that he "had courageously and in the face of certain destruction led his command in a torpedo attack against the enemy."[19]

Ring was not the only Midway warrior who continued after the war to sit alone in an ocean of doubt, hoping to be rescued. In a conference on Midway held in Pensacola in 1988, a tall, retired navy captain rose up in the back of the audience and asked for the floor. What he said is fascinating enough to be listened to at length, as the original audience did:

> I'm Jim Gray. I was skipper of the *Enterprise* fighters, and I'd like to put in a word or two about where were the fighters in the Battle of Midway if somebody would like to hear the answer to that one. I've never had an opportunity to explain what the fighters were doing, instead of being down amongst the torpedo planes when they were getting shot down.
>
> [MODERATOR] After 46 years, sir, you are now having your opportunity.
>
> [GRAY] The only experience we had to build on at Midway was the Coral Sea. The torpedo planes went in safely, the dive bombers and the fighters of the Coral Sea took a pasting. The squadron commander—I think Dick Best was there—greetings, Dick, after 46 years—Wade Mc-Clusky, our group commander, Miles Browning, the staff operations officer, said the best thing for the fighters to do, go to high altitude so they could come down to the torpedo planes' defense if they gave a signal.
>
> Coming back from the Coral Sea, we didn't get into the battle, but we were down there. We were taken into Pearl Harbor, and we traded in our F4F-4 [F4F-3] aircraft for F4F-4s. The F4F-4 had six machine guns, two more than we were used to, had armor plate. We didn't

have armor plate, except some homemade stuff we put in. And the self-sealing tanks, hundreds of pounds of extra weight added on. My squadron and aircraft, as I remember, circled over Torpedo Eight. I know they were Torpedo Eight because they had 15 planes and I couldn't find my other outfit, which was 13 [fourteen actually], I believe. When we got to altitude, there were no Zeros there; they had all gone down and not followed their example of the Coral Sea.

We were at about 20,000 feet. I looked at my gas gauge, and expecting to see I had about a quarter of a tank gone, actually I had about a quarter of a tank left. I started to fly in 1928, I soloed and got my license in 1930. One of the first things I learned about flying in an airplane was only an idiot runs out of gas in an airplane. If I went down to mix it up, all of us would have landed out of gas. I had enough gas to get home, nothing more. So I elected to go home and refuel. Furthermore, the approach of Torpedo Eight was made, and I haven't talked to George Gay about this. . . . We lost the Torpedo Eight people under the overcast, and that was the last I heard of them and knew about it til I saw my gas gauge, and we got the hell out of there to get gas. We went back, and we lived to fight another day. . . . We were up at altitude, and we ran ourselves out of gas getting up there. Sorry about that.

[MODERATOR] Thank you, sir. We appreciate that.[20]

This is what Jim Gray made of his Midway performance in forty some years of mulling it over. The tone of what he had come to believe is pretty well captured in the concluding words of his statement, "Sorry about that." He had changed his mind over the years, for now he says he knew that he was watching Torpedo 8, not Torpedo 6, and now it is his new and heavier plane, the Wildcat F4F-4, that is at fault, consuming gas at an unanticipated rate that made it necessary for him to return to base without helping the torpedo planes. In his original after-action report he stated, however, that he had circled for an hour above the enemy fleet, without any sense of being low on gas apparently, and returned to his ship since the dive-bombers had not appeared and he had not heard any call for help from Torpedo 6: "A prearranged call for help from Torpedo Squadron Six was not given. Our dive bombing groups missed their objective and by 1010 had not commenced their attack. As we had patrolled over the Japanese fleet for one hour it was definitely established that there were no fighters in sight or guarding the dive approach of our bombers. Due to approaching the limits of our fuel this fact was announced over the air and the escort returned to the *Enterprise*."[21] Gray's after-action report was dated June 8, day four after the disaster, and by then Gray must have known that the Japanese Zeroes he didn't see were down shooting up the torpedo planes, and that he had followed Torpedo 8 rather than Torpedo 6 to the target, and that he was circling lazily at 20,000 feet when the torpedo planes made their dreadful run.

There is something deeply sad about these old warriors never able satisfactorily to explain what they did, to themselves or others, but it is a relief to turn to survivors whose reactions were less self-interested. At the Waldron house in Norfolk in June 1942,

> One morning while my mother was on a trip, and not aware of any battle, the mail came. I was only 12 and not in the habit of opening my parents' mail, but while looking for a letter from my father I noticed a letter from the U.S.S. *Hornet.* It was one I had never seen before. It looked very official. I didn't hesitate to open it — something told me it was important. It told the sad story of my father's squadron going into battle and not returning to the carrier. Our maid called my mother's best friend with the news and she in turn called my mother. Mother came home and the usual telegram was there to greet her.[22]

Many of the families of the torpedo squadron members found it hard to believe that their loved ones were gone, and there were those like Oswald Gaynier's wife, Rita, who refused for years, if ever, to believe that her husband was dead. Whitey Moore's intended wife, Betty, married another Midway aviator, Melvin Roach, who himself died in 1944 as a result of a plane crash. She never forgave "Tex" Gay for surviving when her intended did not, and a long time after the war she still, "with a lot of . . . expletives," described him as "a braggart, and a liar, who could not be trusted."[23]

Years later I wrote a book about life in the wartime navy, *Crossing the Line,* and among the letters I received afterward there was the following:

> May 15, 1996
> Dear Mr. Kernan,
> I am the widow of John Wiley Brock, who was in your squadron at one time. He was in VT-6 on the old *Enterprise,* and was killed in May [*sic*] of 1942 at Midway. There is a picture of him with the squadron in your book. What I would like to know, is do you remember him? I have never found anyone who did. I would like this info for our son Jerry Allan Brock, who never knew his father. It's very important to him, and to me also. I know that all the years that have passed dim memories. I am a classic example. But if you remember anything on a more personal level, I would greatly appreciate it. . . . Looking forward to hearing from you, if you have the time and recollect anything about Brock.
> Sincerely,
> Dee Rodrigues

I had to write back that unhappily I could remember little. Then a stroke of luck. I happened to mention the letter to an old shipmate, Dan Vanderhoof, who lives in Olympia, Washington. Dan knew everyone, and he just happened to have been a good friend of John Brock, who began as an enlisted naval aviation pilot but was commissioned just before the war.

Your mention of the touching letter from the wife of John Brock really struck a chord with me. Remembering well when John first appeared in his dress whites as a brand new Ensign. How very proud he was of that uniform. A squadron beer party was held sometime in August or September of 1941 in the vicinity of Koko Head Beach. I took my old Eastman Kodak box camera, and among the pictures was one of John Brock. Stranger than Fiction. Dan

Dan of course got in touch with Dee Rodrigues and told her everything he could remember. She was delighted.

7 Feb, 1997

Dear Dan,

What an absolute joy to receive your letter, to say nothing of the surprise! I'm at a loss for the right words to express my gratitude for you in sharing your memories of John Wiley. You are the first person in all these years who had done so. While reading your letter, that feeling of deja vu and being transported back in time and place came over me. Also that sense of knowing that no one ever dies, as long as they are remembered. Retelling stories and sharing experiences of our generation, keeps all our lost friends and loved ones alive, even through we may have moved on long ago.

We were unique, as subsequent generations have proved . . . in our courage, music and being united as a country.

I dropped out after President Kennedy was killed and became an ex-patriot, living all over the world for years. No regrets.

Dee Rodrigues

The search for survivors goes on still. In 1998 a National Geographic Society expedition located and filmed, 3 miles down in the Pacific Ocean, the hulk of the old *Yorktown,* still looking quite poised, though a bit off-center. It had been battered by bombs and aerial torpedoes on June 4 and then hit by submarine torpedoes that finally put it down on June 7. But in the ocean depths it continues to look almost fit to sail away to another battle. Its sister ship at Midway, the *Hornet,* sank on October 26, 1942, northeast of Guadalcanal, and after the war the *Enterprise,* having gone through nearly every major engagement on the long road to Tokyo, was broken up for scrap. Its stern plate with the ship's name was salvaged and rests in a park in River Vale in northern New Jersey. Take the last exit north on the Garden State Parkway.

The war ended in apocalypse, a fiery conflagration that reduced the Japanese empire to little more than nothing. To the survivors of Midway, it should have been revenge without a shadow. But the very power of it overwhelmed, making the survivors and all the people who had died along the way, like the torpedo crews at Midway, seem small and insignificant, the way Commander Fuchida remembered them: "tiny dark specks in the blue sky, a little above the horizon, on *Akagi*'s starboard bow. The distant wings flashed in the sun. Occasionally one of the specks burst into a spark of flame and trailed black smoke as it fell into the water, so distant as to be only black dots bursting into flame and trailing smoke into the water."[24]

In 1992 wreaths were put in these waters to commemorate what had happened there fifty years earlier, but they floated on the ocean surface, like our memories. Ensign Gay's ashes were spread on the waters, and the *Yorktown* was located and photographed miles down in the ocean. Later the U.S. Navy made Midway Day, June 4, the official commemorative day of the American navy, like Trafalgar Day in Britain. But Dee Rodrigues gets closest, I think, to the best way to rescue our vanished dead: "No one ever dies, as long as they are remembered. Retelling stories and sharing experiences of our generation, keeps all our lost friends and loved ones alive, even through we may have moved on long ago." It is my hope that this story of what actually happened to the torpedo squadrons at Midway will contribute something to keeping those brave men and old shipmates alive.

APPENDIX I

Torpedo Squadron Three

LT CDR E. E. Massey / L. E. Perry, ACRM

Chief Aviation Pilot W. G. Esders / R. B. Brazier, ARM2c

MACH H. L. Corl / L. E. Childers, ARM3c

LT(jg) C. W. Howard / H. L. Lundy, Jr., ARM1c

ENS L. L. Smith / R. Darce, ARM3c

CH MACH J. W. Haas / W. A. Phillips, Jr., ARM3c

LT P. H. Hart / J. R. Cole, ARM1c

ENS D. J. Roche / C. L. Moore, ARM3c

ENS C. A. Osberg / R. M. Hanson, ARM3c

LT(jg) R. W. Suesens / T. L. Barkley, ARM2c

ENS O. A. Powers / J. E. Mandeville, SEA2c

ENS W. E. Osmus / B. R. Dodson, Jr., ARM3c

Torpedo Squadron Six

LT CDR E. E. Lindsey / C. T. Granat, ACRM

LT(jg) S. L. Rombach / W. E. Glenn, ARM2c

ENS E. Heck, Jr. / D. L. Ritchey, ARM3c

LT(jg) J. T. Eversole / J. U. Lane, RM2c

LT(jg) R. M. Holder / G. Durawa, ARM3c

LT R. E. Laub / W. C. Humphrey, Jr., ARM1c

ENS I. H. McPherson / W. D. Horton, ARM2c

LT A. V. Ely / A. R. Lindgren, RM3c

CH MACH S. B. Smith / W. N. McCoy, SEA2c

ENS E. G. Hodges / J. H. Bates, ARM2c

LT P. J. Riley / E. Mushinski, ARM2c

ENS J. W. Brock / J. M. Blundell ARM2c

LT(jg) L. Thomas / H. F. Littlefield, ARM2c

MACH A. W. Winchell / D. M. Cossitt, ARM3c

Torpedo Squadron Eight

LT CDR J. C. Waldron / H. E. Dobbs, ACRM

LT R. A. Moore / T. H. Pettry, ARM1c

ENS W. R. Evans, Jr. / R. E. Bibb, Jr., ARM3c

ENS H. J. Ellison / G. A. Field, ARM3c

LT(jg) J. D. Woodson / O. D. Creasy, Jr., ARM3c

ENS W. W. Creamer / F. S. Polston, SEA2c

ENS J. P. Gray / M. A. Calkins, ARM2c

ENS U. M. Moore / W. E. Sawhill, ARM3c

LT J. C. Owens, Jr. / A. Maffei, ARM1c

ENS H. P. Kenyon, Jr. / D. L. Clark, ARM2c

LT(jg) G. M. Campbell / R. J. Fisher, ARM2c

ENS J. Miles / A. L. Picou, SEA2c

ENS W. W. Abercrombie / B. P. Phelps, ARM2c

ENS G. W. Teats / H. Martin, ARM2c

ENS G. H. Gay / R. K. Huntington, ARM3c

The Torpedo Plane Crews from Midway

LT L. K. Fieberling / ENS J. Wilke/ A. R. Osborn, RM2c

ENS C. E. Brannon / W. C. Lawe AMM3c / C. E. Fair, AOM3c

ENS A. K. Earnest / H. H. Ferrier, ARM3c / J. D. Manning, SEA1c

ENS V. A. Lewis/ N. L. Carr, AMM3c / J. W. Mehltretter, EM3c

ENS O. J. Gaynier / ENS J. M. Hissem/ H. W. Pitt, SEA1c

NAP D. "D" Woodside / A. T. Meuer, PTR2c / L. J. Ogeron, AOM3c

The B-26 Crews, Listed by Plane

69th Bombardment Squadron (Medium)

38th Bombardment Group

CAPT James F. Collins, Jr.
2ndLT Colin O. Villanes
2ndLT Thomas N. Weems, Jr.
SGT Ernest M. Mohon, Jr.
SGT Jack D. Dunn
TSGT Raymond S. White
CPL John D. Joyce

1stLT William S. Watson
2ndLT L.H. Whittington
2ndLT John P. Schuman
SGT James E. Via
SSGT Richard C. Decker
CPL Albert E. Owen
CPL Bernard C. Sietz

18th Reconnaissance Squadron (Medium)

22nd Bombardment Group

1stLT James P. Muri
2ndLT Pren L. Moore
2ndLT William W. Moore
2ndLT Russell H. Johnson
TSGT John J. Gogo
CPL Frank L. Melo, Jr.
PFC Earl D. Ashley

1stLT Herbert C. Mayes
2ndLT Garett H. McCallister

FLIGHT PERSONNEL

2ndLT William D. Hargis
2ndLT Gerald J. Barnicle
SSGT Salvatore Battaglia
PVT Benjamin F. Huffstickler
PVT Roy W. Walters

APPENDIX 2

Four torpedo groups attacked the Japanese at Midway. Torpedo Squadron Three (VT-3) on the *Yorktown,* Torpedo Squadron Six (VT-6) aboard the *Enterprise,* Torpedo Squadron Eight (VT-8) on the *Hornet,* and a scratch Midway Torpedo group consisting of six planes of a detached Torpedo 8 flying the new TBFs, plus four army B-26s modified to carry a torpedo. The after-action reports that spell out the timing of the attacks are not always clear or absent contradictions, but the following amalgamation of the information provides the timing of the main events:

0430 *Kido Butai* launches half its aircraft to attack Midway.

0530 Patrol PBY from Midway radios that it has sighted *Kido Butai.*

0607 Fletcher orders Spruance to "proceed southwesterly and attack enemy carriers as soon as definitely located."

0615 Midway torpedo group takes off.

0702 *Hornet* commences launching its strike.

0706 *Enterprise* begins launching its strike.

0710 Midway torpedo group attacks.

0728 *Kido Butai* hears Japanese scout plane, no. 4 from *Tone,* "sighted what appears to be the enemy composed of 10 (ships), bearing 10 degrees, distance 240 miles from Midway on course 150 degrees, speed 20 knots," the first Japanese knowledge that American fleet is on their flank. (*Japanese Story of the Battle of Midway,* 7. Other Japanese communications copied in appendix 2 are from same source.)

0746 *Hornet* completes launch, torpedo planes being last to take off, and *Hornet* air group departs about 0755 on course of 265 degrees. *Enterprise* strike force leaves in three separate groups by 0806.

0816 Torpedo 8 breaks off from *Hornet* air group to fly a course of 231–234 degrees.

0820 *Tone* no. 4 scout reports that "the enemy is accompanied by what appears to be a carrier."

0840 *Yorktown* launching and dispatching strike.

0855 Search plane messages *Kido Butai,* "Sight 10 enemy attack [Torpedo 8] planes heading toward you."

0917 *Kido Butai* completes taking aboard Midway attack units, turns northeast to 70 degrees and goes to 30 knots.

0918 Torpedo 8, fifteen planes, sighted by *Kido Butai,* 52 degrees to starboard, distance 21 miles. Smoke screen is laid down, and *Akagi* begins evasive action.

0925 Torpedo 8 attacking.

0940 *Akagi* sights "14 enemy planes [Torpedo 6] in position bearing 140 degrees to port, elevation 1 degree, distance 40,000 meters." (*Japanese Story of the Battle of Midway,* 18.) Although Laub, the senior surviving officer of VT-6, says in his after-action report that Torpedo 6 was the first to attack the Japanese, it was sighted by the Japanese 22 minutes after Torpedo 8.

1000 Torpedo 6 attacking *Kaga.*

1010 Fighting 6, ten planes, radios that it has been over enemy for an hour at 20,000 feet and, having seen no enemy fighters, is returning to *Enterprise.*

1015 Torpedo 3, twelve planes, is sighted by *Akagi,* "bearing 170 degrees to port, elevation 2 degrees, distance 45,000 meters." (*Japanese Story of the Battle of Midway,* 19.) Esders reported that Torpedo 3 had sighted three columns of smoke at 0935 to the northwest. Corl, however, placed the sighting at 1000, which is closer to the Japanese report.

1025 McClusky and Leslie arrive with dive-bombers and begin attack.

1030 Torpedo 3 moves north to shift its target to *Hiryu* and begins attack.

APPENDIX 3

A controversy has gathered over the years about the course Commander Stanhope Ring flew with his *Hornet* air group on the first morning of the Midway battle. The plain fact is that whatever route he took, he missed the enemy fleet altogether and lost nearly half of his planes. This failure was grievous, for he led one-third of the limited American carrier striking power that day, and had his dive-bombers attacked before or with the *Enterprise* and *Yorktown* groups, the fourth Japanese carrier, *Hiryu,* would likely not have survived to launch the counterattack that led to the sinking of the *Yorktown.*

At the time the American carriers launched their strikes on June 4, *Kido Butai* was located to the southwest, at about 240 degrees, 160 nautical miles, and approximately 90 minutes' flying time for an air group trying to stay together for a combined strike. Without spelling out the exact course, Marc Mitscher in his after-action report, Ring in his "Letter," and George Gay in his *Sole Survivor* all have the *Hornet* air group flying a southwesterly course, implying that it corresponded to the 240-degree bearing. This course is drawn on the spurious map (see fig. 10), attached to the *Hornet* after-action report, on which no specific headings are given.

Over time, however, evidence has accumulated, largely from the work of Bowen Weisheit, that the Ring group flew off on 265, too far north to have any chance of finding Nagumo (see fig. 11). The weight of the evidence for this course seems conclusive. The late Rear Admiral Walter Rodee, who at Midway was the skipper of Scouting 8, reluctantly revealed in an interview with Bowen Weisheit (*Last Flight,* 88) that the *Hornet* strike group had flown the course written in his logbook, 265 degrees. Eyewitness testimony from the *Hornet* air crews agrees that Waldron turned left, not right, when he broke off, confirming that Ring was north of the Japanese carriers. Here is one of the radiomen in a Scouting 8 dive-bomber: "About a half hour or so after we had all joined up in a wide scouting line I observed VT-8 heading about 40 degrees to our port. I have no real idea of the true heading and I mentioned to Don Kirkpatrick, my pilot, about the new heading that Waldron had taken" (Richard Woodson, "Waldron's Course," BOMRT, posting of March 4, 2004). *Hornet*'s radar plotted a returning flight of Rodee's squadron at 260 degrees, which would make sense only if they had flown out on something like that same heading.

Unfortunately no after-action reports exist for any of the *Hornet* squadrons or its air group, which is, of course, highly suspect in itself since filing was mandatory. Ensign, later Captain, Roy Gee, a pilot in VB-8 who flew on the June 4 mission, recalled that there was wide disagreement about the proper course and that the course finally settled on, Ring's choice, did not correspond to that plotted by others: "CHAG (Commander, *Hornet* Air Group: Stanhope C. Ring) had his own navigation solution, as did our VB-8 CO, LCDR Ruff Johnson, the VS-8 CO, LCDR Walt Rodee, and the VT-8 CO, LCDR John Waldron. The VF-8 CO, LCDR Mitchell remarked that he would use the solution that was chosen. The squadron COs' solutions were different from CHAG's, but he overruled them and said that Air Group 8 would fly his navigational solution. LCDR Waldron strongly disagreed" (Roy Gee, "Remembering Midway"). It is necessary to record, however, that more than sixty years later one of Commander Ring's two wingmen on that fatal morning, Ensign Clayton Fisher, though not sure, remembered matters differently:

I wish I could remember the initial navigational heading the *Hornet* dive bombers used the morning of June 4. To my knowledge the same estimated location of the Japanese carriers was given to all our air group commanders. I flew wing on the *Hornet*'s air group commander. There were no navigational problems, we all had plotted in the enemy's estimated position and knew what course heading we would be flying. If CHAG had decided to fly a different course than what we plotted in our ready rooms I would have been aware of the new course. When we arrived at the estimated position of the carriers I thought they were farther north. Layers of broken stratus clouds we had been flying over were now behind us. We had unlimited visibility and I could see a single large column of very black smoke I thought was from Midway Island. (Clayton Fisher, BOMRT, posting of 2/24/04, Re 265-18, Re *Hornet* Air Group at Battle of Midway).

Fisher was there and his evidence cannot be easily dismissed.

Waldron was convinced, however, that Ring's course was too far to the north, and, "Around 0815, ENS Tappan (VS-8) and ENS Guillory (VB-8) heard Waldron when he broke radio silence. . . . They recalled [in postwar interviews] that he told Ring that they were headed in the wrong direction, and that he knew where the Japanese were. ENS Tallman, flying at the rear of VF-8, observed, like Woodson, the TBDs when they broke away to the left on a course of 234. Supposedly this was in the direction of the IJN carriers as given by the air-plot officer at time of takeoff. The break in radio silence was confirmed by LCDR Foster, Air Operations Officer on the *Hornet,* in his report of June 12, page 4, Item 3. (d)" (Bill Price, BOMRT, posting of August 8, 2003).

The Japanese reports of the battle say "that Waldron's formation came in from almost dead ahead," which would have been the case only if they had arrived on a southerly, rather than a northerly, course. Gay records that the moon was dead center in his windshield on this flight, which could have been the case only on a southwesterly course.

By now the accumulated evidence has convinced most historians, professional and amateur, that Ring undoubtedly took something like a 265-degree course out about 225 miles, with Torpedo 8 breaking off about 0830, Fighting 8 breaking off about 0900 for lack of gas and Bombing 8 turning left a little later by itself south toward Midway. The downed fighter pilots were picked up by the PBYs in the area plotted by Weisheit, not in that given on the map attached to the Mitscher report.

Ring never acknowledged that he took the 265-degree course, so his wide deviation from the bearing to *Kido Butai* has been left hanging without a motive. His friends have said that he expected Nagumo to turn north and wanted to intercept him. Some have even suggested that his compass may have been faulty as a result of the amount of iron in bombs and ammunition he was carrying. In contrast, his critics have pointed out that he was leading a poorly trained air group from a new ship, was rusty as a pilot and navigator, and was probably excited in the circumstances and disoriented. Ring's enemies, and he had many then and now, say that he was trying to avoid the battle.

APPENDIX 4

GAS CONSUMPTION IN THE TBD

A mimeographed chart from 1942, without provenance but likely from Torpedo Squadron Six, of TBD-1 fuel capacity and endurance shows in the "torpedo loaded" column that the plane could carry only 96 gallons of gas with the 2,200-pound load, as compared to its full capacity of 180 gallons. The late Commander Tom Cheek, who had been a TBD pilot before he went to fighters, wrote in a private e-mail that the plane was so underpowered that when you loaded it with over a ton of torpedo, the fuel weight had to be sharply reduced. At a speed of 100 miles an hour with a torpedo aboard and at sea level, meaning no climb for altitude, consumption is said on the chart to be 28 gallons per hour and endurance to be 3.4 hours. This means that the *Hornet* and *Enterprise* torpedo squadrons at Midway, launched 155 miles distant from *Kido Butai,* would be cutting it very close to get to the target and back. Of course, on the return trip, if there was one, without a torpedo fuel consumption would go down, according to the chart, to 25 gallons per hour. But, going in the other direction, some fuel would also have been used in forming up after takeoff, flying in formation, and reaching the 3,000 feet or so of altitude absolutely needed to get up speed for the run-in to attack. During combat, "balls to the walls" consumption would have gone up to 65 gallons an hour to achieve, on the chart only, a speed of 150 knots.

Winds have also to be taken into account, and throughout the day the American carriers, but not the Japanese, had to turn away from the enemy to head into the southeasterly light winds while launching the air group. There were a multitude of factors affecting gas consumption, including the acquired skill of the pilots in leaning out the mixture which most of the Torpedo 8 pilots lacked. Put it all together and the TBDs at Midway would have been worried about gas all the time they were in the air, and the four *Enterprise* and two

Yorktown Devastators that made it back must have been running on empty at the end of their flight. "Pilots, including myself," said Tom Cheek, "leaned their fuel mixtures to the point that the engine was running on fumes rather than solid fuel. . . . Both VT-3 pilots [the survivors, Esders and Corl] told me later that they had been gauge wise running on empty long before they sighted the carrier" (personal e-mail, April 17, 2004). In his after-action report Esders estimates that from being hit he lost 55 gallons of fuel in his port tank, and he gives his time in the air as three hours from the time he took off until his fuel gauge read empty and he saw his home ship. Of course, 55 gallons is just a guess, and suspiciously identical to the contents of a barrel, so he may have just been rounding off. Corl had serious engine trouble after being hit, and he gives his time in the air as three hours and forty minutes.

Waldron's citation for the Navy Cross says, "Grimly aware of the hazardous consequences of flying without fighter protection and with insufficient fuel to return to his carrier. . . ." George Gay says, "He [Waldron] certainly knew we were flying beyond our endurance to get back to our ship, but we might make it close to or even all the way to Midway Island." ("The Skipper," 307).

But others, notably John Lundstrom, do not believe that a TBD carrying a torpedo was on a suicide mission at Midway. Norman Sterrie, a TBD pilot on the *Lexington* at Coral Sea, where the distance for the attack on the *Shokaku* on May 8 was 170 miles, said that his

> log book showed that he was airborne for 5.1 hours, with a torpedo aboard for more than half of that time. He indicated that the Japanese were not where they were expected, and some searching was in order. He further stated that he could not possibly imagine taking off with anything less than a full load of fuel, even with a torpedo aboard. Sterrie further volunteered that for one reason or another, squadron C.O. Jimmy Brett didn't drop his torpedo on his first run at Coral Sea, so Sterrie joined up on Brett's wing for a second run-in on the Japs to deflect firepower, even though he'd dropped his own fish on his first run! He also told me that he "wouldn't ever do *that* again." Norm Sterrie

became a doctor of medicine after he left the Navy. He is 87 years old and in reasonably good health. (Frank DeLorenzo, BOMRT, posting of August 16, 2004)

It's hard to argue with a man who actually made one of those perilous runs, but as in so many things about Midway, the evidence is mixed, and the weight of the evidence is that on every occasion when Devastators loaded with a torpedo took off on an attack of any distance over 100 miles there was great concern about their endurance as well as about the efficiency of their torpedoes. By comparison Kate, the Japanese torpedo plane, could carry 317 gallons in her tanks, which made possible the long-range attacks she regularly made without sweat.

NOTES

ONE

The Destruction of the American Battle Line at Pearl Harbor

1. Layton, *"And I Was There,"* 39.
2. Prange, Goldstein, and Dillon, Miracle at Midway, 48.

TWO

Trading Armor for Speed

1. Fuchida and Okumiya, *Midway, the Battle That Doomed Japan,* 145.
2. Peattie, *Sunburst,* 54.
3. Wildenberg, "Midway, Sheer Luck or Better Doctrine," argues that American tactical practices emphasizing carrier scouting were largely responsible for the American victory. But it is hard to see how it affected our success when the only scouts launched from carriers during the battle were a group from *Yorktown* that searched early to the northwest and found nothing. The Japanese scouts from the cruisers and battleship were duly launched and missed the American carriers only by a mechanical failure.
4. Navy Department, Bureau of Ships, "U.S.S. *Hornet* (CV8) Loss in Action," 32.
5. Buckmaster, "Battle of Midway: 4–7 June 1942."
6. The *Lexington* had electrical generator rooms on either side of central turbines, so that a torpedo hit on one side would be unlikely to cut off all propulsion. When it was hit at the Coral Sea by two torpedoes, it was able to maintain way until a gasoline explosion set it on fire and forced the crew to abandon ship.
7. Belote and Belote, *Titans of the Seas,* 151.

THREE

Obsolete "Devastators" and Obsolescent "Wildcats"

1. Mears, *Carrier Combat,* 3.
2. The amount of gas the TBD could carry with a torpedo on board has been a matter of considerable debate. For an extended view of the evidence and the problem, see appendix 4.
3. Gay, "Skipper," 307. "He [Waldron] certainly knew we were flying beyond our endurance, to get back to our ship, but we might make it close to or even all the way to Midway Island."
4. Cheek, "Ring of Coral."

FOUR

Duds

1. Tillman, *TBD Devastator Units,* 45.
2. Belote and Belote, *Titans of the Seas,* 26.
3. Gay, "Interview," 1.
4. Commander Tom Cheek, a pilot in VT-2 at that time, quoted in Tillman, *TBD Devastator Units,* 34.
5. Gunderson, "History of Naval Torpedo Tracking Ranges," app. A, 73.
6. Childers, letter to Lundstrom, 2.
7. Altogether seven torpedoes are said to have hit the *Shoho,* but in light of the dismal performance of the torpedo pilots and their torpedoes elsewhere at this time, I believe that the number of hits and explosions must have been greatly exaggerated.
8. Belote and Belote, *Titans of the Seas,* 79.
9. Despite their remarkable successes the Japanese were doubtful about their own performance with torpedoes. "During the middle part of May [1942] mock torpedo attacks were carried out, with judges from the Yokosuka Air Group acting as referees. The records during these tests were so disappointing that some were moved to comment that it was almost a mystery how men with such poor ability could have obtained such brilliant results as they had in the Coral Sea. On 18 May, actual tests were made

against CruDiv 8 traveling at high speed. In spite of the fact that the speed was 30 knots with only 45-degree turns, the records made by the fliers were again exceedingly poor. With water depth at 40 to 50 meters, about a third of the torpedoes were lost." *Japanese Story of the Battle of Midway,* 8.

10. Laub, "Torpedo Plane Operations," 2.

11. Gay, *Sole Survivor,* 170–71.

12. Mears, *Carrier Combat,* 53–54.

13. Roscoe, *United States Submarine Operations,* 123.

14. Roscoe, *United States Submarine Operations,* 124.

15. Fuchida and Okumiya, *Midway, the Battle That Doomed Japan,* 220. The timing and details of this submarine attack got hopelessly mixed up by both sides, but the official *Japanese Report of the Battle of Midway* is clear that there was a hit on *Kaga* at 1410 and notes "no damage sustained." The report goes on to specify "induced explosions in gasoline or bomb storage compartments" as the cause of *Kaga*'s sinking.

16. Layton, *"And I Was There,"* 472. The *Hiyo* was not sunk until June 1944, by an aerial torpedo.

17. Belote and Belote, *Titans of the Seas,* 142. It is hard to believe that the Mark 6 magnetic exploder was still being used after all the trouble it had given in the submarine torpedoes, but inertia is as deadly in bureaucracies as in mechanical contrivances.

18. Gannon, *Hellions of the Deep,* 179.

FIVE

Indians and "Ringknockers"

1. Goodrich, *Delilah,* 83.

2. Goodrich, *Delilah,* 31.

3. All officers and enlisted men who flew at Midway in torpedo planes are listed in appendix 1.

4. Clay Fisher, "Re Stanhope Ring," Battle of Midway Roundtable (hereafter BOMRT), posting of February 27, 2001.

5. Waldron's mother was Jane Van Meter, daughter of Mary Aungie, who was the child of a Colonel Dixon and an unnamed Indian woman.

6. A handwritten six pages on her father, c. 1976, by Nancy Waldron LeDrew are deposited in the South Dakota Hall of Fame, Chamberlain, S.D. Quotations attributed to her are all from this unpaginated document.

7. Alice Philip Ward, née Palmer, who worked for Waldron in New York in 1940 before marrying his nephew, Major Robert Philip USMC, who was killed in a plane crash in Samoa in 1943. Robert's brother, George Philip, Jr., the commander of a destroyer, was lost at Okinawa when his ship was hit by a kamikaze.

8. Personal letter from Waldron's great nephew, Greg Philip, February 9, 2004.

9. Mears, *Carrier Combat,* 44.

10. Mears, *Carrier Combat,* 73.

11. Biographical summary deposited in the South Dakota Historical Society in Pierre.

12. Gay, "Interview," 5.

13. Gay, *Sole Survivor,* 125.

14. Mears, *Carrier Combat,* 45.

15. "Officers assigned this derisive appellation are those who take themselves and their roles in the well-defined navy society quite seriously, and are quick to remind others of their real or self-perceived exalted status." Ewing, *Reaper Leader,* 267.

16. Lundstrom, *First Team,* 313.

17. Clay Fisher, BOMRT, posting of June 18, 2004.

18. The citation for the medal makes no mention of his failed attack against the Japanese carriers and refers only to a later attack on cruisers on June 6, which Widhelm rather than Ring led. Even this Ring had marred by over-flying his target on the first run and hitting the gun button instead of the bomb release when he dived again.

SIX

Attack

1. The fliers from VP-24 were Lieutenant D. C. Davis, Ensign G. O. Propst, Lieutenant W. L. Richards, and Ensign A. Rothenberg.

2. Prange, Goldstein, and Dillon, *Miracle at Midway,* 176.

3. Gay, "Interview," 2.

4. Mears, *Carrier Combat,* 46.

5. Wendt, *True Story,* 4.

6. Rose, *Ship That Held the Line,* 126.

7. Lloyd Childers, BOMRT, posting of April 22, 2003.

8. Commander Ferrier—he had a distinguished later career in the navy— was unable to confirm in an e-mail exchange that these planes were using the improved Mark 13, Mod. 2, torpedo that his group had practiced with in Narragansett Bay. See Ferrier, *Torpedo 8, the Other Squadron.*

9. Fuchida and Okumiya, *Midway, the Battle That Doomed Japan,* 193. He was writing in 1955 and the order of attack got mixed up in his memories. He has four TBFs attacking first, and then six B-26s. There were in fact six TBFs followed by four B-26s.

10. Ferrier, *Torpedo 8, the Other Squadron,* 74.

11. Cant, *America's Navy,* 226. Cant interviewed crewmembers when the two surviving B-26s returned to Hickham Field, Oahu, shortly after the battle.

12. Cant, *America's Navy,* 227.

13. Cant, *America's Navy,* 226.

14. Cant, *America's Navy,* 227.

15. Cant, *America's Navy,* 227–28.

16. Lundstrom, *First Team,* 332. Whether this message permitted Spruance the delay he then took is still debated. It would seem that the message of 0603 had already "definitely located" the Japanese. But Fletcher, who had been suckered in the Coral Sea, may have wanted to hold back the strike lest the Japanese be hiding a second group of ships.

17. Cressman et al., *Glorious Page,* 84.

18. Roy Gee, "Books of Interest," BOMRT, posting of January 28, 2005.

19. The *Hornet* group course remains a matter of great contention. For a full discussion, see appendix 3.

20. Waldron talked to Ring on radio before separating, breaking radio silence, of course, but when Ring refused to change course, Waldron told him to go to hell and flew off on a course of 234 degrees. No copy of the exchange exists, but it was overheard by Lieutenant Troy Guillory and corroborated by Ensign Ben Tappan, both of whom were interviewed and taped by Weisheit, *Last Flight,* 44ff.

21. Buckmaster, "Battle of Midway: 4–7 June 1942."

22. Gray explained long after the war "that he knew he was over Torpedo Squadron 8 as he could count their 15 planes and knew that VT-6 had launched fewer." U.S. Naval Institute Professional Seminar Series, "The Battle of Midway and Its Implications," 14. But in his action report, June 8, 1942, four days after the action, Gray still had himself over Torpedo 6.

23. Rose, *Ship That Held the Line,* 129–30, quoting Quillen's report, attached to Mitscher's after-action report. Waldron used his own first name to identify his first division. "Johnny Two" is likely to have been Lieutenant James C. Owens, Jr., who led the second division. Dobbs was, of course, Waldron's radio/gunner.

24. Fuchida and Okumiya, *Midway, the Battle That Doomed Japan,* 208–9.

25. Gay, *Sole Survivor,* 125–26.

26. Laub, "Torpedo Plane Operations." See fig. 9 for his drawing of the attack on the *Kaga.*

27. Esders's watch, or his memory, was about half an hour or more slow. The other survivor of this attack, Machinist Harry Corl, gives the correct times.

28. Esders, "After-Action Report," 1.

29. Childers, letter to Lundstrom.

30. Fuchida and Okumiya, *Midway, the Battle That Doomed Japan,* 209–10.

31. Prange, Goldstein, and Dillon, *Miracle at Midway,* 260 and reference.

32. Cheek, "Ring of Coral." Cheek added, "When the *Akagi* exploded I was looking at it broad on the port, the first sign of an explosion was a small whitish-yellow spot at what appeared the waterline level that is what gave

me the impression it may have been a torpedo. The explosion that instantly followed, judging from its greasy yellow-green color, I judged to be a magazine. It seemed I was looking right into the guts of the ship."

33. Gay, "The Skipper," 108.

34. See Parshall and Tully, *Shattered Sword.*

SEVEN
"The Best-Laid Schemes o' Mice an' Men Gang Aft Agley"

1. Raymond A. Spruance, "Foreword," to Fuchida and Okumiya, *Midway, the Battle That Doomed Japan,* 8.

2. Murray, "Battle of Midway: 4–7 June 1942," 3.

3. Nimitz, "Battle of Midway: 4–7 June 1942," 14.

4. Laub, "Torpedo Plane Operations," 4.

5. Ewing, in Cressman et al., *Glorious Page,* 191.

6. Gay, *Sole Survivor,* 115.

7. This was Ensign C. Markland Kelly, Jr., whom to commemorate—he was not picked up—Bowen Weisheit wrote his remarkable reconstruction of the flight, setting the record straight on "the flight to nowhere" after forty years of official obscurity.

8. Cheek, "Ring of Coral."

9. Prange, Goldstein, and Dillon, *Miracle at Midway,* 255.

10. A vivid description of this desperate action is provided by Commander Tom Cheek, a warrant officer at the time flying a Wildcat. See Cheek, "Ring of Coral."

11. Regan, *In Bitter Tempest,* 157.

12. Mitscher was sworn in as a rear admiral during the voyage but continued to function as captain until his ship returned to port.

13. Browning, who gave orders for the strike of both *Enterprise* and *Hornet,* did not provide such critical information as the designated target, a group course, or an option course for the other carrier. He was perhaps in the midst of a breakdown, getting into shouting matches with other officers

on the bridge. See Clark G. Reynolds, in Cressman et al., *Glorious Page*, 214–16.

14. Gay, "Interview," 2.

15. See appendix 3. Ring may have chosen this or another course on the bridge, but 265 degrees is now believed to be the course he actually led his group on the attack.

16. Ring said in his explanatory letter years later that "departure from *Hornet* was taken on pre-estimated interception course" but then implied that he had flown south of the Japanese fleet: "VT-8 and the *Enterprise* group made contact with the enemy north of the point at which I turned south." Linder, *"Lost Letter,"* 31, 32.

17. Mitscher, "Battle of Midway: 4–7 June 1942," 2.

EIGHT

"Sorry about That"

1. Barde, "Midway: Tarnished Victory," 188. Osmus was assumed dead in the attack, and these facts did not come out until after the war, when a war crimes commission questioned Japanese survivors.

2. Barde, "Midway: Tarnished Victory," 189, describes what Osmus told his captors, which was a lot, but points out that the new pilots of VT-3, of which Osmus was one, had been given no instructions on how to respond if captured and questioned.

3. James Bowen, BOMRT, posting of February 16, 2004.

4. Two other American airmen, Ensign Frank W. O'Flaherty and his radioman, Bruno Gaido, from Scouting 6, were shot down while dive-bombing the Japanese fleet and were picked up by the destroyer *Makigumo*. They were interrogated and killed on orders from the fleet command. The captain of the *Makigumo* thought that spilling their blood on board would be unlucky, so cans filled with water were tied to their legs, and they were thrown overboard to drown. It is satisfying to note that bad luck was not avoided. *Makigumo* hit a mine and sank near Guadalcanal in early 1943.

5. History seemed from the outset to ignore that the detached Torpedo 8 flying out of Midway had two survivors, Ensign Earnest and his radioman, Ferrier. "Meet the third sole survivor of Torpedo 8," Ferrier, who stayed in service and retired a commander, reportedly said in a speech long after the war.

6. Gay, *Sole Survivor,* 105.

7. "Frenchy Fayle (not with VT-8 at Midway, in hospital at Pearl with a machete wound of, according to the surviving members of VT-8, very questionable origin)" reads the caption to Fayle's picture on-line at the Web site "Torpedo 8: In Color" (http://www.centuryinter.net/midway/Carrier_Squadrons/Torpedo_Eight/in_color.html). Fayle was not alone in his problem. McClusky's radioman, a chief petty officer, missed what would have been the greatest event of his life when he reported to the group commander before takeoff that he had broken his glasses, didn't have another pair, and couldn't see a thing without them.

8. I am indebted to William Roy, BOMRT, posting Re: 111–27, for this information, including the location of the motel as "on east highway 41, just past the Collier County courthouse."

9. Lundstrom added also that, like Walter Lord, he would have preferred to be on the bridge of the SS *Californian* rather than the *Titanic* when that mighty ship went down within sight of the *Californian,* whose crew did not respond to the repeated distress signals.

10. Standard Bureau of Areonautics form for after-action reports.

11. He had, of course, neither reversed nor retired but turned to 70 degrees to attack the American fleet.

12. Mitscher, "Battle of Midway: 4–7 June 1942," 6. Since the success of the mission depended on it, even radio silence does not seem a good enough reason for the information not to be sent to Ring. But there is considerable doubt about whether the *Hornet* or any other ship in the fleet received such a message. If there were such a message, it would have been one of the messages of 0952 and 1000 from Gray over the Japanese fleet, which were sent after the Japanese knew of the American carriers' presence.

13. "I think there was conscious deception in the Hornet action report, deliberate omissions in the narrative and outright fraud in the attached sketch. What's interesting in the next Hornet action report, for 5 Oct. 42 raid on Buin-Shortland, there are not only group & squadron reports, but the XO's statement notes the composition of the meals that were served prior to launch! Somebody had let it be known there'd better be more accountability." John Lundstrom, private e-mail to author.

14. Flunking out on his first try at Annapolis, he used political pull to get him an unusual second chance. Altogether it took him six years to graduate third from bottom in his class.

15. Taylor, *Magnificent Mitscher,* 163.

16. Linder, "Lost Letter," 31.

17. "About one hour after the planes had departed the enemy reversed his course and started his retirement. We did not break radio silence to report this to the planes." Mitscher, *Battle of Midway,* 6.

18. Linder, "Lost Letter," 32. Ring's assumption that the *Enterprise* planes had information the *Hornet* group lacked must have been known to be wrong by the time he wrote the letter. The *Enterprise* dive-bombers flew too far south on their first leg of a course of approximately 230 degrees but found the enemy in their further search northward. Torpedo 6 also arrived to the south of the Japanese but saw smoke and found them.

19. Linder, "Lost Letter," 33.

20. U.S. Naval Institute Professional Seminar Series, "Battle of Midway and Its Implications."

21. Gray, J. S., Jr., "Report of Action."

22. Nancy Waldron LeDew, letter about Waldron.

23. James O'Reilly, BOMRT, posting of July 10, 2002.

24. Fuchida and Okumiya, *Midway, the Battle That Doomed Japan,* 208.

BIBLIOGRAPHY

Published Sources

Barde, Robert E. "Midway: Tarnished Victory." *Journal of Military Affairs,* December 1983, 188–92.

Belote, James H., and William M. Belote. *Titans of the Seas: The Development and Operations of Japanese and American Carrier Task Forces during World War II.* New York: Harper and Row, 1975.

Buell, Thomas S. *The Quiet Warrior: A Biography of Admiral Raymond A. Spruance.* Boston: Little, Brown, 1974.

Burgerud, Eric. *Fire in the Sky: The Air War in the South Pacific.* Boulder, Colo.: Westview, 2000.

Cant, Gilbert. *America's Navy in World War II.* New York: J. Day, 1943.

Chesneau, Roger. *Aircraft Carriers of the World, 1914 to the Present: An Illustrated Encyclopedia.* Annapolis, Md.: Naval Institute Press, 1984.

Craven, Wesley Frank, and James Lea Cate. *The Army Air Forces in World War II.* Vol. 1: *Plans and Early Operations, January 1939 to August 1942.* Chicago: University of Chicago Press, 1948 [see esp. "Midway," 451–62].

Cressman, Robert J., Steve Ewing, Barrett Tillman, Mike Horan, Clark Reynolds, and Steve Cohen. *A Glorious Page in Our History: The Battle of Midway 4–6 June 1942.* Missoula, Mont.: Pictorial Histories, 1990.

Daws, Gavan. *Prisoners of the Japanese: POWs of World War II in the Pacific.* New York: William Morrow, 1994.

Esders, Wilhelm G. "Torpedo 3 and the Devastator—A Pilot's Recollection." *The Hook,* August 1990, 35–36.

Ewing, Steve. *Reaper Leader: The Life of Jimmy Flatley.* Annapolis, Md.: Naval Institute Press, 2002.

———. *Thach Weave: The Life of Jimmie Thach.* Annapolis, Md.: Naval Institute Press, 2004.

Falk, Lieutenant Commander Brian G., USN. "What Went Wrong at Midway?" *Naval Institute Proceedings,* June 1, 2001, 134–38.

Ferrier, H. H. "Torpedo Squadron Eight, the Other Chapter." *U.S. Naval Institute Proceedings,* October 1964, 72–76.

Friedman, Norman. *U. S. Aircraft Carriers: An Illustrated Design History.* Plans by A. D. Baker III. Annapolis, Md.: Naval Institute Press, 1983.

———. *U.S. Naval Weapons.* Annapolis, Md.: Naval Institute Press, 1983.

Fuchida, Commander Mitsuo, and Masatake Okumiya. *Midway, the Battle That Doomed Japan: The Japanese Navy's Story.* Edited by Clarke H. Kawakami and Roger Pineau, with a foreword by Raymond A. Spruance. Annapolis, Md.: Naval Institute Press, 1955; reprint ed. used here, 2001.

Gannon, Robert. *Hellions of the Deep: The Development of American Torpedoes in World War II.* University Park: Pennsylvania State University Press, 1996.

Gay, George. "The Skipper—Torpedo 8." *Shipmate,* June–July 1966, 303–8.

———. *Sole Survivor: The Battle of Midway and Its Effect on His Life.* Naples, Fla.: Naples Ad/Graphics Services, 1979.

———. "Torpedo 8: One Man's Story." *Frontier,* July 1981, 48–51.

Goodrich, Marcus. *Delilah.* New York: Farrar and Rinehart, 1941. Reprint, Time-Life Books, used here, 1981.

Kernan, Alvin. *Crossing the Line: A Bluejacket's World War II Odyssey.* Annapolis, Md.: Naval Institute Press, 1994.

Knott, Dick. "Night Torpedo Attack." *Naval Aviation News,* June 1982, 10–13.

Layton, Edwin T., with Roger Pineau and John Costello. *"And I Was There": Pearl Harbor and Midway—Breaking the Secrets.* New York: William Morrow, 1985.

Lewin, Ronald. *The American Magic: Codes, Ciphers, and the Defeat of Japan.* New York: Farrar, Straus and Giroux, 1982.

Linder, Captain Bruce R. "Lost Letter of Midway." *Naval Institute Proceedings,* August 1999, 29–35. [Excerpts from Admiral Ring's manuscript, which was dated March 1946, are printed among extended comments and interpretations by Linder. To my knowledge the entire letter has never been made public.]

Lord, Albert. *Incredible Victory.* New York: Harper and Row, 1967. Reprint, Perennial, used here, 1993.

Lundstrom, John. *Black Shoe Carrier Admiral: Frank Jack Fletcher and the Pacific Fleet, 1941–42.* Annapolis, Md.: Naval Institute Press, 2006.

———. *The First Team: Pacific Naval Air Combat from Pearl Harbor to Midway.* Annapolis, Md.: Naval Institute Press, 1990.

Mears, Frederick. *Carrier Combat.* New York: Doubleday, Doran, 1944.

Milford, Frederick J. "US Navy Torpedoes." *Submarine Review,* October 1996, pts. 2 and 3.

Morison, Rear Admiral Samuel Eliot. *History of United States Naval Operations in World War II.* Vol. 4: *Coral Sea, Midway, and Submarine Actions, May 1942–August 1942.* Boston: Little, Brown, 1949.

Morris, Frank D. "Four Fliers from Midway." *Collier's,* July 25, 1942, 23–26.

Parshall, Jonathan, and Andrew Tully. *Shattered Sword: The Japanese Story of the Battle of Midway.* Washington, D.C.: Potomac Books, 2005.

Peattie, Mark R. *Sunburst: The Rise of Japanese Naval Air Power, 1909–41.* Annapolis, Md.: Naval Institute Press, 2001.

Prange, Gordon W., Donald M. Goldstein, and Katherine V. Dillon. *Miracle at Midway.* New York: McGraw-Hill, 1982.

Regan, Stephen D. *In Bitter Tempest: The Biography of Admiral Frank Jack Fletcher.* Ames: Iowa State University Press, 1994. [Many serious errors. A command study of Fletcher will be published by John Lundstrom c. 2006.]

Roscoe, Theodore. *United States Submarine Operations in World War II.* Annapolis, Md.: Naval Institute Press, 1949. [See esp. ch. 20 for a history of the torpedo problem.]

Rose, Lisle Abbot. *The Ship That Held the Line: The U.S.S. "Hornet" and the First Year of the Pacific War.* Annapolis, Md.: Naval Institute Press, 2002. [Flawed by many factual errors.]

Sanger, Grant. "Freedom of the Press or Treason?" *Naval Institute Proceedings,* September 1977, 96–97.

Taylor, Theodore. *The Magnificent Mitscher.* Foreword by Admiral Arthur W.

Radford, Introduction by Jeffrey G. Barlow. Annapolis, Md.: Naval Institute Press, 1991.

Tillman, Barrett. *TBD Devastator Units of the US Navy.* Osprey Combat Aircraft 20. Oxford: Osprey, 2000.

Ugaki, Admiral Matome. *Fading Victory: The Diary of Admiral Matome Ugaki, 1941–1945.* Foreword by Gordon W. Prange. Translated by Masatak Chihaya, Donald M. Goldstein, and Katherine V. Dillon. Pittsburgh, Pa.: University of Pittsburgh Press, 1991.

U.S. Naval Institute Professional Seminar Series. "The Battle of Midway and Its Implications." Pamphlet. U.S. Naval Institute, Annapolis, Md., May 6, 1988.

Weisheit, Bowen. *The Last Flight of Ensign C. Markland Kelly, Junior, USNR, Battle of Midway, June 4, 1942.* Privately printed. Baltimore: Ensign C. Markland Kelly, Jr. Memorial Foundation, 1993, 1996.

Wendt, Lloyd. "The True Story of Heroic Squadron 8." *Chicago Sunday Tribune,* May 30, 1948, 4–5.

Wheeler, Howard. "With Earnest at Midway." *Naval Aviation News,* June 1982, 22–23.

Wolfert, Ira. *Torpedo 8: The Story of Swede Larsen's Bomber Squadron.* Boston: Houghton Mifflin, 1943.

Unpublished Letters, Reports, and Midway Action Reports, Including On-Line Web Sources, with URL Addresses

Battle of Midway Round Table (BOMRT). http://www.midway42.org. This remarkable on-line discussion group is composed of veterans of the battle — including a number who flew in the attacks — naval personnel who were not present, and many people simply interested in the details of Midway. Founded by Bill Price and ably carried on by Ron Russell, the accumulated exchanges this group has assembled provide an extraordinary database of the Midway battle.

Buckmaster, Captain Elliot. "Battle of Midway: 4–7 June 1942, Online Action Reports: Commanding Officer, USS *Yorktown,* of 18 June, 1942." http://www .history.navy.mil/docs/wwii/mid7.htm.

Cheek, Commander Tom. "A Ring of Coral," 2003. Battle of Midway Roundtable. Veterans' Stories. http://home.comcast.net/~r2russ/midway/ring
coral.htm.

Childers, Lloyd. Unpublished letter, December 3, 1974, in collection of John
Lundstrom.

———. Speech presented at Golden Gate Wing "Ghost Squadron" Prop-Talk,
January 1998. Recorded by John Crump. http://www.ghostsquadron-ggw
.org/proptalk/speaker.cfm?date=199801&name=Lloyd%20Childer.

Corl, Machinist Harry. "After-Action Report." Naval Historical Center, Washington Navy Yard, Washington, D.C.

Esders, Chief Aviation Pilot, Wilhelm G. "After-Action Report." Naval Historical Center, Washington Navy Yard, Washington, D.C.

Fletcher, Admiral Frank Jack. "Battle of Midway: 4–7 June 1942, Online Action
Reports: Commander Cruisers, Pacific Fleet of 14 June 1942." http://www
.history.navy.mil/docs/wwii/mid3.htm.

Gay, Ensign George, USNR. "Interview." World War II Interviews, box 11,
pp. 1–14. Operational Archives Branch, Naval Historical Center.http://www
.history.navy.mil/faqs/faq81-8c.htm.

Gee, Captain Roy. "Remembering Midway." Battle of Midway Roundtable.
Veterans' Stories. http://home.comcast.net/~r2russ/midway/vets_stories_
gee.htm.

Gray, J. S., Jr. "Report of Action 4–6 June 1942." June 8, 1942. A16–3. Naval
Historical Center, Washington Navy Yard, Washington, D.C.

Gunderson, Charles R. "The History of the Naval Torpedo Tracking Ranges
at Keyport." Measurement Technologies Division, Naval Undersea Warfare
Center Division, Keyport, Wash. Prepared for the Naval Undersea Museum,
Keyport, Wash., August 1998.

The Japanese Story of the Battle of Midway. U.S. Navy, Office of Naval Intelligence. OPNAV P32-1002. June 1947. Navy Department Library. http://www/
history.navy.mil/library/special/midway.htm. [The Japanese chronology of
the battle.]

Laub, R. E. Lt. (jg) USN. "Attack on Japanese Task Force, June 4, 1942." VT-

6/A5-2/ECA (029). June 4, 1942. After-action report of Senior Surviving Officer, Torpedo Squadron Six. Naval Historical Center, Washington Navy Yard, Washington, D.C.

———. "Torpedo Plane Operations in the Air Battle of Midway, June 4, 1942." June 21, 1942. Naval Historical Center, Washington Navy Yard, Washington, D.C. [A description of the major failures of the torpedo planes and their weapon.]

LeDew, Nancy Waldron. Undated letter, c. 1976, about her father, Lieutenant Commander John Waldron. Six handwritten pages, deposited at the South Dakota Hall of Fame, Chamberlain.

Mitscher, Admiral Marc. "Battle of Midway: 4–7 June 1942, Online Action Reports: Commanding Officer, USS *Hornet,* Serial 0018 of 13 June 1942." http://www.history.navy.mil/docs/wwii/mid5.htm.

Murray, Captain J. D. "Battle of Midway: 4–7 June 1942, Online Action Reports: Commanding Officer, USS *Enterprise,* Serial 0133 of 8 June 1942." http://www.history.navy.mil/docs/wwii/mid6.htm.

Navy Department. Bureau of Ships. "U.S.S. *Hornet* (CV8) Loss in Action, Santa Cruz 26 October, 1942." *War Damage Report No. 30,* Navships 30 (374), July 8, 1943.

Nimitz, Admiral Chester A. "Battle of Midway: 4–7 June 1942, Online Action Reports: Commander in Chief, Pacific Fleet, Serial 01849 of 28 June 1942." http://www.history.navy.mil/docs/wwii/mid1.htm.

Ofstie, Rear Admiral Ralph A. "Report of Action, 4 June 1942, by Ensign G. H. Gay USNR." *Memorandum to the Commander in Chief, [Admiral Ernest King,]* June 7, 1942. Naval Historical Center, Washington Navy Yard, Washington, D.C. [Made at King's request. Ofstie was the senior naval member, U.S. Strategic Bombing Survey, after the war.]

South Dakota Historical Collections, compiled by the State Historical Society. Folder "John C. Waldron, XIII, 1946." http://www.sdhistory.org.

Spruance, Admiral Raymond A. "Battle of Midway: 4–7 June 1942, Online Action Reports: Commander Task Force Sixteen, Serial 0144A of 16 June 1942." http://www.history.navy.mil/docs/wwii/mid4.htm.

Vanderhoof, Dan. Personal letters, undated, c. 1994–2000, in the possession
  of the author.
Wildenberg, Thomas. "Midway, Sheer Luck or Better Doctrine?" Naval
  War College Press, Newport, R.I., 2004. http://www.nwc.navy.mil/press/Re
  view/2005/Winter/art6-w05.htm.
Woodson, Richard, "Waldron's Course," BOMRT, posting of March 4, 2004.

INDEX

Page numbers in italics refer to illustrations